Praise for the first edition of
Winter Trails: Vermont and New Hampshire

"An excellent guide! Keep *Winter Trails* in your backpack. Marty Basch
is your 'personal guide' to the trails of Vermont and New Hampshire.
Complete, concise, and elegantly descriptive!"

—Jim Radtke, editor-in-chief, *The Snowshoer* magazine

"*Winter Trails: Vermont and New Hampshire* is a user-friendly guide that
will lead cross-country skiers and snowshoers to some of the best
snow and most scenic landscapes in the East."

—David Goodman, contributing editor, *Ski, Powder,*
and *Backcountry* magazines

"You'll appreciate this guide's at-a-glance practicality and its engaging
depictions of each trip's unique features. . . . By paying snowshoeing
its due, this guide helps a new segment of outdoor adventurers enjoy
the winter's glory."

—Jason Brady, publisher, *Northeast Adventure Magazine*

Help Us Keep This Guide Up to Date

Every effort has been made by the author and editors to make this guide as accurate and useful as possible. However, many things can change after a guide is published—new products and information become available, regulations change, techniques evolve, etc.

We would love to hear from you concerning your experiences with this guide and how you feel it could be improved and be kept up to date. While we may not be able to respond to all comments and suggestions, we'll take them to heart and we'll make certain to share them with the author. Please send your comments and suggestions to the following address:

The Globe Pequot Press
Reader Response/Editorial Department
P.O. Box 480
Guilford, CT 06437

Or you may e-mail us at:
editorial@globe-pequot.com

Thanks for your input, and happy travels!

A **FALCON** GUIDE®

WINTER TRAILS™ SERIES

winter trails™

Vermont & New Hampshire

The Best Cross-Country Ski
& Snowshoe Trails

Second Edition

MARTY BASCH

FALCON®

GUILFORD, CONNECTICUT
AN IMPRINT OF THE GLOBE PEQUOT PRESS

A FALCON GUIDE®

Copyright © 1999, 2002 by Marty Basch
Previously published by Falcon Publishing, Inc.

Cover photographs: Dennis Curran
Cover and interior design: Nancy Freeborn
Trail maps created by Equator Graphics © The Globe Pequot Press
State maps: Lisa Reneson
Photo credits: pages xvii, 62, by Jan Duprey; 116, courtesy of Waterville Valley Resort; all other photos by Marty Basch.

ISBN 0-7627-1052-7
ISSN 1536-6146

Library of Congress Cataloging-in-Publication Data is available.

Printed in the United States of America
Second Edition/Second Printing

CAUTION
The Globe Pequot Press assumes no liability for accidents happening to or injuries sustained by readers who engage in the activities described in this book.

To Jan Duprey,

Sunshine on a winter's day.

Vermont

Contents

Acknowledgments, x

Introduction, xi

vermont

1. Osmore Pond Loop, 2

2. Nebraska Notch, 6

3. Indian Brook Park Loop, 9

4. Sam's Run, 11

5. Stowe Recreation Path, 15

6. Slayton Pasture Cabin/Haul Road Loop (Trapp Family Lodge), 18

7. Edson Hill, 21

8. Wiessner Woods, 25

9. Robert Frost Interpretive Trail, 29

10. Maple Loop/Bolton Valley, 32

11. Camel's Hump View Trail, 35

12. Burrows Trail, 38

13. Faulkner Trail, 41

14. Hogback Trail, 45

15. South Ridge Loop, 49

16. Lost Horizon Loop, 52

17. Merck Forest and Farmland Center's Birch Pond Loop, 55

18. Little Michigan/Stone Place Trails Loop, 59

19. Grout Pond Loop Trail, 63

20. Big Bear Loop, 66

21. Mount Olga Trail, 69

22. Old Railroad Bed/West River Trail, 73

New Hampshire

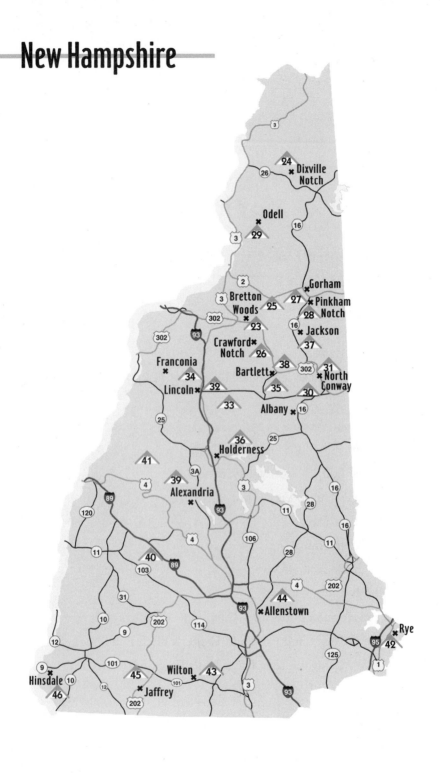

new hampshire

23. B&M Trail, 78
24. Canal Trail, 82
25. Hayes Copp Ski Trail/Leavitt's Link, 86
26. Mount Willard Trail, 89
27. Nineteen-Mile Brook Trail, 93
28. Great Angel Loop/Great Glen Trails, 97
29. Fire Tower Trail, 101
30. Boulder Loop Trail, 104
31. Echo Lake Trail, 107
32. Lincoln Woods/Pemi East Side Road Trails, 110
33. North End Loop, 113
34. Around-Lonesome-Lake Trail, 117
35. Lower Nanamocomuck Ski Trail, 121
36. Old Bridle Path, 125
37. Ellis River Trail, 128
38. Upper Saco River Loop, 132
39. Cardigan Loop, 135
40. Cascade Loop, 138
41. Holts Ledge, 141
42. Battery Seaman Loop, 144
43. Heald Pond Trail, 147
44. Bear Brook State Park Loop, 150
45. Mount Monadnock Loop, 154
46. Kilburn Loop, 158
    Appendix, 162
        Vermont Ski Centers, 162
        New Hampshire Ski Centers, 165
        Resources, 167
    Bibliography, 169
    About the Author, 171

Acknowledgments

Over the rivers and through the woods in winter can be an exhilarating experience. Though it's nice to have company, either physically, or in spirit. Thanks to the following people who were most helpful in either accompanying me or pointing the way during the research and updating of this book: Jan Duprey, Steve and Brian Finch, Paula Brisco, Jane Reilly, Elizabeth Taylor, Chris Morrison of The Balsams, Ben Wilcox at Bretton Woods, the Appalachian Mountain Club's Rob Burbank, Jackson Ski Touring's Thom Perkins, Kathleen Murphy at Tubbs Snowshoes, Colin Lawson at Grafton Ponds, both Michael Walsh and Andrew Zboray of Monadnock State Park, Charlie Yerrick at Trapp's, Tony Clark at Blueberry Hill, Mike Miller at Mountain Meadows, Heidi White and Bill Altenburg at Phillips Brook Recreation, John Wiggin at Woodstock, John Brodhead at Craftsbury Common, Kathleen Fitzgerald at Stowe Land Trust, Mike Seeger, Walt Stockwell and Stacy Lopes at Waterville Valley, Norsk's John Chiarella, Zach Leonard at Edson Hill Manor, Jim Tabor in Stowe, and Don Cochrane and Maria Caron at Mountain Top for lending me a two-way radio during a most memorable ski in a Vermont nor'easter.

Introduction

Welcome to winter!

Miles and miles of trails wind through the snow-encrusted forests, mountains, and valleys of Vermont and New Hampshire. Nature centers, state parks, national forests, community recreation areas, downhill and cross-country ski areas, open fields, and your own backyards all provide access to winter trails.

Trails that by summer take hikers to the summit of a 4,000-footer or meander gently around a pond reflecting the autumn sun become paths to ply for cross-country skiers and snowshoers.

Those who love winter know the silence of a trek in solitary woods. They see the beauty after a snowfall in a pine forest. They know the bugs are gone and there are fewer people. The cold doesn't bother them. Instead it becomes a challenge unto itself.

Those who love winter also know about the dangers that lurk around the bend. Changing weather, sudden squalls, flimsy ice, and more can turn a nice day into a survival test.

For those who prefer human-powered transportation, winter is a time for cross-country skiing and snowshoeing. Each mode of travel has its own benefits. If you can walk, you can snowshoe. If you can walk, you can cross-country ski, too, but it might take considerably more effort. Nonetheless, experiencing winter can be enjoyable.

Vermont and New Hampshire are home to a multitude of winter trails. The outings in this book cover trips in the Green Mountain National Forest in Vermont and the White Mountain National Forest of New Hampshire. There are also excursions through state parks, conservancy lands, and cross-country ski areas. Most of the outings do not have a fee, though trail passes may be required at the cross-country ski areas. In 1996 the White Mountain National Forest instituted a program that requires users to purchase a recreation pass when parking at trailheads within the forest boundaries.

Skiers and snowshoers aren't the only recreationists using the winter trails. You will also encounter hikers and snowmobilers on certain outings. Trails that are used by snowmobilers are kept at an absolute minimum in this book.

Each outing is rated for difficulty, has driving directions to the trailhead and trail directions, offers suggestions for last minute groceries, places to stay, where to rent equipment, and a post-trip meal, comes with helpful phone numbers, and provides the distance of each journey. The trips can take a full day or just a couple of hours.

However you wander the trails of winter, stay sharp and enjoy.

Equipment

Technology marches on. If you are paying any attention to what you strap to your feet, you'll see that snowshoe and cross-country ski equipment has made a bit of a leap since its early days, when the Vikings or Eskimos romped through the woods and across the tundra.

Don't fret. The old stuff still works. Those wooden ash snowshoes over the fireplace, in the attic, or on the wall of the garage will still do the trick. So will those three-pin skinny skis you bought at a yard sale on a whim a decade or so ago. Actually, if you tackle some of the trails in the White Mountains suggested in this book, be sure to stop in at Baldy's on the Kancamagus Highway and ask to see the snowshoe museum in the back. You'll see some excellent examples of what people used to use in the snow.

Wooden snowshoes with the basic bear-paw design are still being made, but the shape of the snowshoe has changed to become more streamlined. There is more choice as far as bindings go, and the snowshoe has become more lightweight. Modern-day snowshoes are also coming with affixed crampons, fingerlike plates that prevent slipping.

If you are new to snowshoeing and not sure if you are going to like it, the best bet is to rent a pair of snowshoes at a sporting goods store or cross-country ski center. Don't be afraid to pepper the staff with questions. That's what they are there for.

A snowshoer prepares her gear to tackle Mount Tom in Woodstock, Vermont.

How do you choose the right snowshoe for you? There is a three-step process based on snow conditions, terrain, body weight, and price.

The first thing to do is figure out what kind of snowshoeing you plan to do. Most activity falls into either a recreational or mountaineering category. Recreational snowshoeing revolves around family outings, walking, running, hiking, aerobic cross-training, and day treks. These are the activities usually done on easy, broken trails. Mountaineering centers around wilderness excursions, overnight adventures, climbing approaches, and steep terrain. These outings are usually done in varying conditions from deep powder to unbroken trails to windswept snow.

Next, figure out your total body weight. That's not just how much you weigh, but the weight of the total package—body, clothing, and anticipated weight of backpacks.

The last step is to compare snowshoes. Based on how you expect to use them, take a look around the store. Ask about prices. Sample the various bindings to figure out which one will work best for you. Remember, the outdoors in winter will be a lot colder than a retail store. Make sure the equipment you buy is easy to use.

Some snowshoers use ski poles while on a trek. They are useful during ascents and descents. Lean on them if a tree isn't available.

Choosing the right cross-country ski equipment is a bit more complicated because you must purchase skis, boots, bindings, and poles. Basically, you can choose from waxable or waxless skis that are used for recreational or backcountry skiing. Of course, groups have subcategories that are based on weight, ability, style, and terrain. Nordic skiers also must decide if they want a ski for skating or the classical technique.

If you just want to get out and back on easy terrain at your local park or cross-country ski area, stick to the waxless skis. They perform well under most conditions, and you don't have to worry about waxing.

Racers and better skiers like waxable skis. They can get more glide out of the ski, which usually means a bit less work. But you must learn the right way to wax them, based on temperature and snow conditions.

As for the type of ski to get, as with snowshoeing, figure out what kind of skiing you want to do. Those skiers who like groomed and tracked trails stick to recreational skis, while those who prefer more untamed conditions gravitate to the wider, stronger-edged skis.

Proper Clothing

Wondering what to wear when heading outside to snowshoe or cross-country ski? Just remember one word—*layers*. Even though it could be downright cold outside, get ready to be quite warm while engaged in activity. You'll cool off quickly when you stop. To dress for comfort, choose lightweight and breathable underwear as a first layer. On top of that have an absorbent layer, like a sweater or fleece. The outside layer should be a wind-resistant shell.

The idea behind dressing this way is to better manage your body's temperature while snowshoeing or skiing. Layering gives you greater control than one thick layer of insulation, like a parka, does. By putting on and taking off layers, you act like a thermostat, regulating the body's temperature. As you exert more energy, your body will start to heat up. When that happens, remove a layer. Cold? Put a layer back on.

The first layer is responsible for your skin. Perspiration is no fun in winter. That's why it's best to stay away from cotton and consider a layer that wicks away wetness from the skin and traps a blanket of dry, warm air. The middle layer has a couple of jobs. One is to encourage the perspiration to get on out of there. The other is to insulate by trapping warm air. Materials like fleece or wool are able to maintain that insulting quality even when wet.

The same principle applies to pants, although, in general, your legs don't need as much insulation as your upper body. Still, the layer next to your skin should be just like that next to the torso. On extremely cold, windy, or rainy days, a shell should be used on top of the insulating layer.

A hat is of primary importance, because the head is a source of heat loss. Cover it to stay warm and dry. Take your hat off to cool down. Gloves and mittens are also part of the proper clothing arsenal. You should wear fleece, wool, or insulated gloves. A fleece glove with an overmitt is excellent on extreme weather days. The choice between gloves or mittens is a personal issue.

Dry and warm feet are happy feet and are essential to an outdoor winter experience. Forget cotton socks. Fleece and wool are the mantra. Some people like two layers of socks, one thin and the other thick. It's your choice.

Cross-country skiers have a couple of choices for their boots. For the most part, low-cut boots are better for groomed trails. Higher boots that go above the ankle offer better support and are usually associated with deeper, ungroomed snow conditions.

Snowshoers and a cross-country skier share the trail on the grounds of the Trapp Family Lodge.

Waterproof hiking boots with decent ankle support should prove well suited for snowshoers. Plastic mountaineering boots can also be used for extended trips. For those casual outings, you can wear almost anything. But the idea is to stay warm and dry, so any rubber, insulated, or hiking boot will suffice.

A few accessories are helpful during an outdoor winter excursion. A neck warmer is an excellent choice. Not only will it keep your neck warm, it can also double as a goofy looking hat, wearable in the solitude of the woods. Your neck warmer can also triple as a headband if it is folded in half. A headband keeps ears warm on those sunny winter days called "spring." Gaiters are also a good idea. They keep the snow from getting in between your boots and socks.

Don't forget about eye protection. On a sunny day, winter's glare can be brilliant to the point of discomfort so consider taking a pair of sunglasses. Though usually associated with downhill skiing and snowboarding, goggles are another good addition particularly for snowshoers heading out on windy days, as blowing and drifting snow can be irritating to the eyes.

Consider a camera or binoculars for capturing those wonderful human and wildlife moments.

Safety

In winter, trail conditions can vary drastically from day to day. Both the Appalachian Mountain Club and the Green Mountain Club agree that when using trails for winter travel, plan ahead. Winter in Vermont and New Hampshire can be unpredictable and severe. Changing weather, dropping temperatures, shorter days, and deep snow are all challenges you'll encounter while skiing or snowshoeing. Breaking trail can be an exhausting experience. If an excursion takes you to higher elevations over open rock faces and above the treeline, snowshoes with crampons are necessary. It is imperative that you take extra warm clothing and a few safety items because winter is rather harsh on mistakes. Though what you carry in a backpack or fanny pack is a personal choice, some suggested items include a guidebook, map, compass, insulated water bottles, high-energy foods, waterproof matches, flashlight with spare batteries (kept warm), rope, duct tape, toilet paper, and ski wax. The cell phone is up to you.

First-aid kits are also recommended. They can include items like pain relief medicine, adhesive bandages, gauze, ace bandages, and antiseptics.

Hypothermia and frostbite are dangerous threats in winter. Hypothermia, considered the leading cause for backcountry emergencies, occurs when the body's core temperature drops below normal. The most important impact of hypothermia is that it impairs judgment. Symptoms include shivering, disorientation, loss of coordination, and slurred speech. In order to prevent hypothermia, wear clothing that keeps you well insulated. Be sure to stay dry. Hydrate. Drink more than you think you need. Keep an eye on the weather. Be cognizant of the conditions of people you are traveling with.

Frostbite is the result of tissue being damaged by severe cold and wind. Pale skin and numbness are the two basic symptoms, though as the condition worsens, the affected area can freeze. Like hypothermia, frostbite can be prevented by wearing proper clothing that provides warmth and allows for flowing circulation. It is important to eat and hydrate well.

Before heading out, always plan ahead. Remember, there is safety in numbers. If you are inexperienced, don't travel alone. Take into consideration the abilities of those in your group, the weather, terrain, and hours of light left in the day. Many outdoor clubs, organizations, schools, and community centers offer first-aid and outside skill courses and workshops. Take one.

Above all, use common sense.

Navigation

Getting lost on a trail in winter is relatively easy. All you have to do is not pay attention and a pleasant day snowshoeing up the side of a 4,000-footer can turn into a race against daylight and disaster. Though beautiful, the whiteness of winter is also deceiving because it blankets landmarks that may be familiar to summer hikers and walkers. The soft and airy flakes can cover a stream where one misstep can plunge you into icy wetness. Stray just a few feet off the main trail and you may find yourself thigh-deep in a cold, hard, snowy trap.

In general it is easy to snowshoe or cross-country ski at a groomed, ski center. Maps are available before heading out, and trails are usually well signed with arrows pointing the way. Many centers have maps along the way, especially at junctions, that indicate where you are within the network. To alleviate any concerns, it is always best to question the frontline warrior behind the desk in the office for the latest information. This helpful person can even outline the route with a transparent marker to allay any fears. Cross-country ski networks are patrolled as well; experienced personnel look for skiers and shoers on the trails before the system shuts down for the day.

To avoid any confusion, always stick to the trail.

In the woods and forests, blazes are the key to successful navigation. Trees are marked at varying intervals with different colored paint. Follow

Some winter trails offer cabins for an overnight stay.

the blazes and you are following the trails. Signs also mark the way. But in winter the snow can either cover or obscure a blaze. Severe storms can throw blowdowns in the path, which can be confusing. And should you be on the Long Trail in Vermont, be particularly alert. The trail was not designed for winter use. It is blazed in white with markings four to five feet above the ground. During periods of soft light and deep snow, these can be hard to spot.

Of course following other people's tracks on the trail makes navigation easy. But if you are trailblazing in unfamiliar terrain, the task increases in difficulty. Rely on yourself and not other people's footsteps. Always look for blazes.

Carry a map and a compass. Know how to use them.

Courtesy

The popularity of snowshoeing has boomed. With such popularity comes the responsibility of courtesy and etiquette for both the snowshoer and skier. Snowshoeing in deep snow is fun, but many like the groomed, compacted trails at a cross-country ski area. There are some areas that forbid snowshoeing on the groomed trails, instead providing snowshoers with trails all their own. However, snowshoers and skiers do share many trails—both in fee areas and in the woods.

Give skiers the right of way. Skiers are generally going faster than snowshoers. Plus it's easier and quicker to get around on snowshoes.

Don't snowshoe on ski tracks. The beauty of the snowshoe is that it can virtually go anywhere. If you are snowshoeing on a skating lane, stay to the right. If possible stick to the edge of the trail and on the deeper snow. Skiing on tracks marred by snowshoe prints is nerve wracking.

Follow the rules. If you are at a ski center, stick to the rules. If in the woods, and a trail says for skiers only, abide by it.

Trail Classification

The outings in the Winter Trails series are based on a three-tier classification system—easiest, more difficult, and most difficult. There aren't any hard-and-fast rules for determining the level of difficulty. In general an outing rated easiest is one that has flat and gentle terrain. It can be done in a couple of hours. A more difficult excursion has more rolling terrain. Better technique is needed to conquer the hills. The distance is a bit longer than on an easy trip. A most difficult outing has the most challenging terrain, requires advanced skill levels, and can be long and/or remote. Elevation can also play a factor.

Please note that a trail that might be easiest on snowshoes is not always easiest on skis. Heading down or up a particular section of a trail on snowshoes is a far different experience than on skis. Consider your outings accordingly.

Key to Icons
cross-country skiing trail
snowshoeing trail
skate skiing (skating) trail

The tracks of a cross-country skier make their way across Osmore Pond.

vermont

Osmore Pond Loop

Groton State Forest, Marshfield, Vermont

Type of trail:	
Also used by:	Hikers
Distance:	3.3 miles
Terrain:	Flat trek along a northern pond
Trail difficulty:	Easiest
Surface quality:	Ungroomed, but skier and snowshoe packed
Food and facilities:	Bring all you need on this loop; food and water are not available. There are several outhouses along the way and three lean-to shelters for overnight accommodations. Onion River Sports in Montpelier (20 Langdon Street, tel. 802–229–9409) has rentals. There is also a picnic area, and good eating at the P and H Truck Stop (802–429–2141) in Well's River.
Phone numbers:	For Vermont State Parks headquarters in Waterbury, call (802) 241–3655.

Though only about a half hour's drive from places like the state capital of Montpelier and St. Johnsbury, Groton State Forest has a remote feel to it. The forest is used by hikers, naturalists, snowmobilers, snowshoers, and cross-country skiers, while supporting four-legged wildlife, such as black bear, moose, deer, mink, and beaver, as well.

There is room for every sort of creature in its 25,000 acres, making it the second-largest contiguous landholding by the state. The forest's history is linked to logging and the railroad. When the Montpelier to Wells River Railroad opened in 1873, it went through the forest. By the 1920s most of the timber was cut. Fire has also ravaged the area. One fire in 1903 put a new spin on the landscape, changing it from spruce, fir, and pine to red maple and birch.

The Civilian Conservation Corps came to the rescue in the 1930s, camping by the shores of Osmore Pond while planting pine and spruce.

The rough topography and poor drainage in this forest is blamed on a glacier that crept through some 10,000 years ago, depositing gravel, sand, silt, and boulders.

A sign for Osmore Pond Loop points the way for the trail around the Vermont pond.

The Osmore Pond Loop is a hiking trail that encircles the shores of the pond for about 2 miles. The path is clearly blazed in blue and has a few wet areas with narrow footbridges to cross. It is an outing made for both the family or those looking for an easy few hours out in the warming winter sun. The three lean-to shelters on the eastern side of the pond make the loop appealing for an overnight stay. The lean-tos each have an outhouse and fire pit, though no water is available. The picnic area on the western side of the pond offers an opportunity for al fresco dining by the water's edge or under the roof of a shelter.

The trailhead, at the entrance to the New Discovery Campground, is well plowed. Park here by the tollgate and head straight on the campground road through the New Discovery Campground. It is on this section of your route that you might meet snowmobiles. Continuing on, the road comes to a junction (there's a portable toilet on the left and a bathhouse on the right). Straight ahead are large blue blazes. Head for them. This is the New Discovery Trail, and it will be the path for about 0.5 mile. The trail heads downhill, passing by a spruce-fir stand, crossing another camp road, and then ending at a junction with the Osmore Pond Loop. The loop can be done in either direction, but we followed the posted arrow and turned right.

Directions at a glance

0.0 Head straight down the campground road through the New Discovery Campground Lot B.

0.2 There is a junction here. The New Discovery Trail, though not signed, is well marked with blue blazes. The trail begins straight and runs between the bathhouse on the right and site 39 on the left.

0.7 Junction with Osmore Pond Loop. Turn right on Osmore Pond Loop.

1.5 Junction with Little Deer Trail, which leaves right. Turn left toward the pond to continue on Osmore Pond Loop (Big Deer Mountain/Lake Groton/ Peacham Pond signs).

1.7 Bear left on Osmore Pond Loop at junction with Hosmer Brook, Big Deer Mountain, and Cold-water Brook Trails.

2.6 Turn right on New Discovery Trail and continue to trailhead.

The Osmore Pond Loop hugs the shore and offers many a fine view of the neighboring hills and peaks. At a few sections the poor drainage is evident as narrow footbridges cross over boggy and marshy areas. It's not too long before you reach the picnic area. The sheltered picnic site is up on a small hill, while other tables are near the pond's edge.

From here, the trail winds along the shore, passing another boggy area that has narrow footbridges. At 0.6 mile from the picnic area the trail crosses under power lines and becomes bumpy but fun. Turn left at the junction with the Little Deer Trail. The Little Deer Trail heads right to the ridge atop the mountain. The Osmore Pond Trail turns left and skirts the southern edge of the pond. A wide bridge crosses the running waters of Hosmer Brook. After the bridge you'll spot the first of the three lean-tos, along with its outhouse.

There are a few wet spots on the eastern side too. A junction with the Hosmer Brook, Big Deer Mountain, and Coldwater Brook Trails is easily navigable.

The three lean-tos are spread out over the remainder of the loop and offer quiet places to rest and enjoy. The trail slices through the woods where giant marshmallows, really glacial boulders covered in snow, line the forest floor. New growth evergreens sprout up.

As the loop continues to the northern tip of the pond, it becomes much wetter, particularly in its final stretch.

You'll experience déjà vu when you encounter the sign for the New Discovery Trail on the right. Turn right and head uphill, following the same path that took you to the pond. It's about 0.7 mile back to the car from here.

How to get there

From Montpelier or St. Johnsbury, travel on Route 2 to Route 232 South. The trailhead is on the left. From Well's River travel on Route 302 to Route 232 South. The trailhead is on the right. The signs in Groton State Forest are not up during winter. The New Discovery Campground, where this loop begins, is about a half mile north from the maintenance department on Route 232. The trailhead is marked by a white house and a plowed area with tollhouse.

Nebraska Notch

Mount Mansfield State Forest, Underhill Center, Vermont

Type of trail:	⬤ ▬
Also used by:	Backcountry skiers, hikers
Distance:	4.3 miles
Terrain:	Hilly ride by a famous face
Trail difficulty:	More difficult
Surface quality:	Ungroomed, but packed by use
Food and facilities:	There are no facilities near the loop; winter campers use Twin Brooks Tenting Area; a brook is the water source, bring a filter to treat water. For food, stock up before you go; there are two general stores at Underhill Center—Underhill Country Store (802–899–4056) and Wells Corner Market (802–899–2418)—for last minute items. The Ski Rack in Burlington at 85 Main Street has rentals (802–658–3313). The Comfort Inn, 1285 Williston Road, South Burlington (802–865–3400), is minutes outside the city.
Phone numbers:	Vermont Department of Forests, Parks and Recreation in Essex Junction on West Street, (802) 879–6565.

Vermont's most famous face may be its highest peak—Mount Mansfield. At 4,393 feet its ridge looks a bit like a human profile, and specific features are given names of human parts, like nose, chin, forehead, and even Adam's apple.

Though this loop does not climb to the summit of the peak, it does utilize the Long Trail, which leads to the top. The Long Trail is a 270-mile-long hiking trail that runs from the Massachusetts-Vermont line to the Canadian border. Maintained by the Green Mountain Club, it has some 175 miles of side trails, too. The Long Trail is actually the oldest long-distance hiking trail in the country, according to the Green Mountain Club. In winter sections of the trail are used for snowshoeing and skiing.

Directions at a glance

0.0 Leave on the Nebraska Notch Trail.

1.7 Turn left on the Long Trail.

3.1 Turn left on the Overland Cross-Country Ski Trail and return 1.2 miles to the parking area.

Three trails make up this loop in the Mount Mansfield State Forest: Nebraska Notch Trail, the Long Trail, and the Overland Cross-Country Ski Trail. As a snowshoe trip, the loop is a moderate undertaking. To complete the entire loop as a backcountry skier, it is best to be at least at an intermediate level.

The Nebraska Notch Trail leaves the trailhead by a sign near the parking lot and is a long, moderate climb. At about 0.1 mile the Overland Cross-Country Ski Trail enters left, but the blue-blazed Nebraska Notch continues upward along a wide swath. Streams flow trailside. You'll cross a log bridge. There is a bit of relief by a clearing where you can spot the 2,979-foot Mount Clark. The Nebraska Notch Trail descends rather nicely along a brook before you cross a bridge (put up by the Underhill/Jericho Boy Scouts in 1991) to the left. Notice the first of a series of beaver ponds. Cross the bridge and begin a steep ascent to a trail junction. You can make a short side trip at the junction with the Long Trail by making a right and heading 0.4 mile through the glacial cirque and walls of Nebraska Notch to the privately owned Taylor Lodge on the Lake Mansfield Trail (a private trout fishing club). Vistas of Lake Mansfield and beyond are the rewards.

Turn left on the white-blazed Long Trail at the sign and head north. The trail rolls along the west side of Mount Dewey; its huge boulders with icy claws are in the distance. It is narrow in places, and there are a few wet spots, including two brooks at 2.9 miles into the trip, and then one about 0.1 mile later. The first two brooks you reach are quick and steep. After the second brook you'll reach the Twin Brooks Tenting Area. Soon after the area, the red-blazed Overland Cross-Country Ski Trail enters. Thanks go to the Civilian Conservation Corps, which built the Overland back in the 1930s. Turn left and begin the long, winding, and mostly wide descent. The Underhill Ski Trail soon enters to the right, but stay left on Overland. The trail will cross a couple of brooks and drainages.

After about 1.1 miles the Overland rejoins the Nebraska Notch Trail and returns to the parking area.

How to get there

From I–89 north take exit 15 east. Travel through Essex Junction, Essex Center, and Jericho. In Underhill Flats turn right at 13.2 miles on River Road. In Underhill Center, at 16.4 miles, turn right on Stevensville Road and follow it about a mile to a skier parking area on the left. The Maple Leaf Farm is a landmark. Stevensville Road continues about another mile to the trailhead for Nebraska Notch, but it is only suitable for four-wheel-drive vehicles. This trip begins there from the well-signed trailhead. Sign in.

A snowshoer signs the log book at the trailhead for the Nebraska Notch Trail.

Indian Brook Park Loop

Essex, Vermont

Type of trail:	🚶 ▬▬
Also used by:	Hikers
Distance:	Nearly 2.0 miles
Terrain:	Flat ramble through the woods and by the water
Trail difficulty:	Easiest
Surface quality:	Ungroomed but packed
Food and facilities:	There are no winter facilities at the conservation area; the nearest food is in Essex Junction: a supermarket (Hannaford) near the junction of Routes 15 and 289. After the jaunt try Martone's Market (802–878–8163) on Main Street, Essex Junction, for deli. For rentals try the Ski Rack, 85 Main Street, Burlington (802–658–3313). For lodging, consider University Inn and Suites, 1 Dorset Street, Burlington (802–863–5541).
Phone numbers:	Essex Parks and Recreation Department, (802) 878–1342.

Circling Indian Brook Reservoir is like taking a leisurely stroll. It is not uncommon to meet locals out for a walk with their dogs on a warm winter afternoon. The trail, which goes around the finger-shaped lake, is never far from the shore, offering panoramas of the frozen water and its various bays. Located in Essex, outside of Vermont's largest city, Burlington, the nearly 2-mile-long loop is easy to ski or snowshoe. Those on skis will find some of the hills exhilarating as well, as the trail rolls up and down in a few sections.

The 66-acre lake is a conservation and public recreation area on a total of 574 acres. The dam, evident near the lake's edge, was built in 1957 so the lake could serve as a water supply.

The counterclockwise loop begins at the summer boat launch area. There is no sign marking the trail, though blue arrows do point the way along the path. The trail initally skirts the shore as it rolls through the forest. Up to the right are rocks that tumbled down when a glacier moved through the area. The trail widens out at about 0.3 mile as it passes by an inlet called Scout's Point. This section of the loop

Directions at a glance

0.0 Leave the unmarked trailhead along the reservoir shores.

0.3 The trail bears right at a blue arrow.

0.6 Turn left at blue arrow.

1.1 Junction with McGee Road. Turn right at arrow.

1.7 Cross road by dam.

1.8 Turn left on Indian Brook Road back to parking area.

Indian Brook Park Loop
Scale: 1:12,000 or 5.28" = 1 mile

N

558

North Bay

Reservoir

Scout's Point

800

700

START/FINISH

600

600

479

is a road that is lined in parts by an old stone wall. The trail leaves the view of the lake and begins to ascend here. The loop takes a big left turn at about the 0.6-mile mark and meanders through a marshy area at the northern tip of the lake, called appropriately enough North Bay.

The northern edge of the loop is hilly as it climbs up on a bit of ridge before rolling back down and toying with coming near and away from the water's edge.

At 1.1 miles there is a signed junction with McGee Road. The trail bears to the left, following the edge of the water. After the junction cross over a tributary and start a gentle ascent away from the water. Glide down as the trail of softwoods and evergreens offers you a view of Thunder Bay. As the trail nears its end, it leaves the woods and comes out near the reservoir's dam. Here it seems to peter out. But it's easy to get back to the trailhead. Cross over the road by the cul-de-sac, and then you'll see the familiar Indian Brook Road. Just turn left and follow the road back to the trailhead.

How to get there

From I–89 north take exit 15 and travel east on Route 15 through Essex Junction. Cross over I–289 and make the first left on Old Stage Road. Make a second left on Indian Brook Road. Follow road into the park and bear right. The road ends at the trailhead near a number of boulders. In summer this is the boat launch. The trailhead is to the left of the rocks.

Sam's Run

Craftsbury Outdoor Center, Craftsbury Common, Vermont

Type of trail:	
Distance:	5 miles
Terrain:	Rolling invigorating trek through farm, field, and forest
Trail difficulty:	Most difficult
Surface quality:	Groomed, single-tracked, skate lane
Food and facilities:	Cross-country ski and snowshoe rentals, lessons, a wax room and snacks for the trails are available at the Nordic ski center. There is also ice skating. Overnight accommodations —two lodges and three cabins—are available. The Craftsbury Outdoor Center serves breakfast, lunch and dinner. There are also snacks. For those who want something else, try the Craftsbury General Store at (802) 586–2811 which serves up sandwiches and has last minute items for the trail.
Phone numbers:	The Craftsbury Outdoor Center is (800) 729–7751.

The far reaches of Vermont's Northeast Kingdom are home to the 65 miles of cross-country ski trails at the Craftsbury Outdoor Center. The trails wander through the woods, with views of rippling hills, and to the picture-perfect town of Craftsbury Common. The community is quintessential Vermont with its snow-covered town green, neat white homes, and vistas to the Black River Valley.

A rustic yet charming atmosphere pervades the Nordic network. Ski through a farm meadow with a classic New England red barn and then wind through the tranquility of the woods and stop at a beaver pond. Snowshoers have over 10 miles of trails for themselves. The Center is also home to the East's only point to point marathon, an annual race which regularly attracts over 500 skiers.

There is much to ski at the center. Ruthie's Run is one that attracts a lot of intermediates, in particular the extension, which provides winter access to the wetland homes of beavers. For those looking to do some miles, the 9.5-mile Grand Tour is the loop to do. The ski takes striders along the Black River and to the Common. A spur allows them to ski into the village for a bite to eat. The circuit continues over a pair of lakes for ever-changing scenery.

Though Sam's Run is marked as a more difficult loop, it really doesn't feel that way. The 5-mile circuit (through open fields, by a river, and through maples that drip sweet sap near spring) is hilly, with long, moderate climbs and downhills. But the beauty of cross-country skiing is ripping down the nicely groomed boulevards after those pushes.

Sam's Run was named, not surprisingly, after a man named Sam. The story goes that Sam was looking for Ruthie's Run, a trail named after a hound dog. Sam got lost and Sam's Run was the trail he made. The loop is also part of the Craftsbury Marathon.

The loop is a figure eight with some roller-coaster rides thrown in. Undergoing a bit of a personality change, the route provides skiers with a chance to frolic in the woods before leading them to the windswept vistas of farm and field with views of the Worcester Range in the distance. There are many sides of Vermont. On Sam's Run, you see several of them.

Directions at a glance

0.0   Leave the touring center and follow signs for Sam's Run. After 50 yards, turn left.

0.3   Turn right on Sam's Run.

0.4   Turn right and soon bear left.

1.0   Stay straight on Sam's Run through junction.

1.1   Bear right on Sam's Run.

2.5   Turn right on Sam's Run.

3.7   Turn right on Sam's Run.

4.4   Stay straight on Sam's Run.

4.8   Turn right on Sam's Run and follow back to touring center.

A farm meadow and a rustic barn await skiers and shoers at Sam's Run.

You'll also see an improved trail system. In the fall of 2000, aluminum signs were erected at the many junctions. The signs are easily visible, have trail numbers, trail name, arrows and, most importantly, the distance back to the touring center. That way, the math is already done for you.

Sam's Run leaves from the touring center and immediately enters the forest, a respite on those days when the wind decides to blow. From pine to hardwoods, the winding trail weaves through the landscape, and boredom won't be a factor here. If skiers aren't whisking down, they're about ready to go up. Through the leafless trees skiers get a glimpse of where the trail goes passing through a patchwork of open fields and patches of evergreens.

The trail deposits skiers in a border zone of forest, farms and fields. Yellow and red farmhouses quietly huddle against a northern winter. The trail opens up to the distant mountain range on the edge of evergreens. Ski in the windswept fields and back into the shelter of nature's limbs for a couple of fast downhills, by frozen beaver swamps, and then a nearly half-mile climb back to the touring center.

How to get there

From Hardwick, follow Route 14 north 8.4 miles and turn right on TH 1 (sign for Craftsbury Outdoor Center). Follow TH 1 about 4 miles and make right on TH 7 (Mill Village Road). Travel TH 7 for 1.3 miles and turn right on TH 12 (Lost Nation Road) and follow it to Craftsbury Outdoor Center. The way from Route 14 is well signed.

Stowe Recreation Path

Stowe, Vermont

Type of trail:	
Also used by:	Walkers
Distance:	5.3 miles one way
Terrain:	Flat
Trail difficulty:	Easiest
Surface quality:	Partially groomed, skier tracked
Food and facilities:	Rental shops on Mountain Road in Stowe have cross-country skis and snowshoes. One is Action Outfitters (802–253–7975). Another is Mountain Sports and Bike Shop (802–253–7919). Lodging is varied. Try the Hob Knob Inn, Mountain Road (802–253–8549). A number of restaurants can be accessed by the Recreation Path; a grocery store, Grand Union, is off Route 100 (Maple Street).
Phone numbers:	Stowe Area Association is (802) 253–7321 or (800) 247–8693.

Stowe and skiing go hand-in-hand. Though the area is known for its diverse alpine slopes, four groomed cross-country ski networks, and miles of backcountry adventures, as well as home to the state's highest peak, there are those days when simple and scenic will do. On those days, the Stowe Recreation Path is the answer.

Directions at a glance

0.0 Leave from the trailhead by the Stowe Community Church.

3.0 The parking area by Luce Hill Road.

3.8 The parking area by Mountain Road.

5.3 The path ends by the covered bridge and Brook Road parking area.

Return along same route.

Flatish and free, the paved path constructed in the early 1980s is a 5.3-mile-long white greenway, utilized by cross-country skiers, snowshoers, and walkers in winter. The small-town atmosphere of Stowe is evident along the path that meanders between the flowing waters of the West Branch River and Stowe's commercial Mountain Road (Route 108). Stowe is a hip place. Yes, dogs are allowed on the path. However, how many other communities make this request of dog owners: "Please suggest to your dogs that they use the woods (the pavement is nicer when kept clean)." The good thing about the path is that it is used by locals. When playing the visitor, locals are your best resource. Be nice and maybe they'll let you in on local skiing and après-ski secrets.

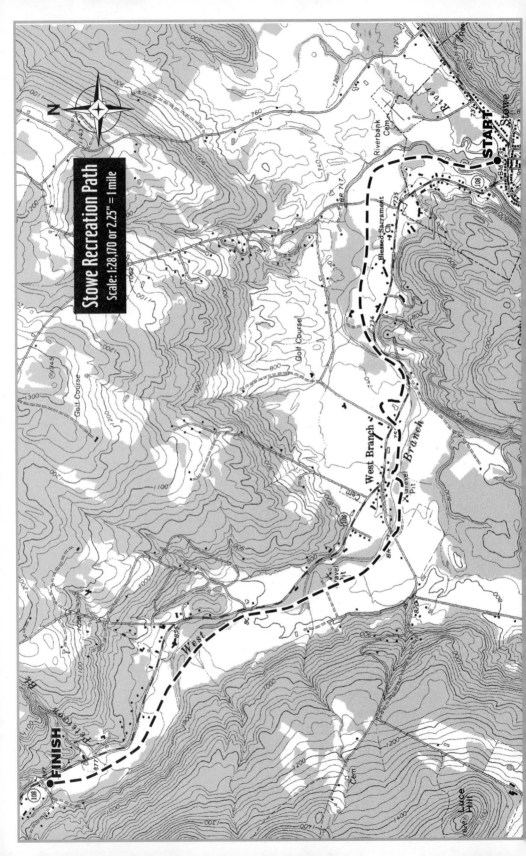

The path begins beside the charming white Stowe Community Church and ends by a red covered bridge spanning the river. In between the greenway winds through and around open fields, woods, quaint inns, incredible vistas of Mount Mansfield, and farms. Take a backpack and stop to shop along the way—the path accesses some of the stores along Mountain Road. Lunch is also a possibility because the path takes you past menus offering everything from fast burgers to prime rib and lobster. Have fun choosing.

The path doesn't take you far from civilization, and certainly the cars on Mountain Road will remind of you of that, but the path does offer its quiet and pastoral moments.

The path begins by the Stowe Community Church, arguably the most photographed building in town. The church was constructed for $12,000 in 1863. Almost immediately, you cross the first of ten bridges along the path. Whether you take off your winter equipment to cross is determined by the type of equipment you have, your confidence, and the amount of snow on that day. Take off your equipment for the road crossings you encounter.

Ski past the scenery along the West River and look up to Mount Mansfield, the highest peak in the state.

There are many fine vistas, and the views of the farm and Mount Mansfield from the Thompson Park bridge are spectacular.

It is not necessary to ski the entire length of the path and return, though that makes a fine outing. Four public parking areas allow users access to the path at different spots, making the trip an out-and-back-to-the-car experience. Aside from the area at the church, the others are on Luce Hill Road (across from the Snowdrift Motel), off Mountain Road by the Alpenrose, and at the end of the path by the red covered bridge on Brook Road.

How to get there

From I–89 take exit 10 and follow Route 100 north about 11 miles to Stowe Village. Route 100 becomes Main Street, and the Recreation Path leaves from the Stowe Community Church.

Slayton Pasture Cabin/Haul Road Loop

Trapp Family Lodge, Stowe, Vermont

Type of trail:	━━ ＜ ●
Distance:	7.2 miles
Terrain:	Flat, rolling, and hilly, a diverse adventure at a first-class trail system
Trail difficulty:	More difficult
Surface quality:	Groomed, single track, double track
Food and facilities:	Rentals (cross-country and snowshoe), lessons, rest rooms, gift shop, a wax room, and more are available at the ski touring center. The Slayton Pasture Cabin, near the loop's halfway mark, is an ideal lunch spot, while Trapp is an ideal place to stay.
Phone numbers:	The Trapp Family Lodge, (802) 253-5719.

The hills above Stowe are alive with cross-country skiing and snowshoeing at the Trapp Family Lodge. The 35 miles of groomed trails (snowshoers are welcome on all of them plus about 4 miles of their own) are at the heart of Stowe's extensive network of some 90 miles of groomed trails. The four centers—Trapp, Edson Hill Manor, Topnotch, and Stowe Mountain Touring Center—in the shadows of impressive Mount Mansfield, are interconnected.

The upscale Trapp Family Lodge takes credit for being the first commercial Nordic center in the United States. In 1968 Johannes von Trapp, whose family inspired the film *The Sound of Music*, started out with a few wooden skis and a Norwegian instructor. The Austrian expatriates never looked back as the resort has grown to attract some 30,000 skiers per year.

Located up in the hills with panoramic views of the Stowe Valley and surrounding mountains, the wide, neatly groomed trails of the network are novice and intermediate friendly. Beginners can stay near the ski center in the lower elevations, making an easy loop along the tree-lined Sugar Road to Russell Knoll Track.

Directions at a glance

0.0 From the ski center take Sugar Road.

1.2 Turn right on Parizo Trail.

2.4 Turn left on Cabin Trail. The Slayton Pasture Cabin is at 3.0 miles.

3.0 Take the Haul Road.

6.9 Haul Road becomes Luce Trail. Follow it 0.3 mile to the ski touring center.

But those seeking more of a challenge and impressive mountain views can try their skill on the Slayton Pasture Cabin/Haul Road Loop.

The Haul Road

Slayton Pasture Cabin

Picnic Knoll

Luce Hill

START/FINISH

Brook

Slayton Pasture Cabin/Haul Road Loop
Scale: 1:20,443 or 1.65" = 1 mile

There is something satisfying and homey about stopping in a rustic log cabin in the woods to rest and refuel with hot drinks, soups, and snacks. Just before the midway point, the Slayton Pasture Cabin provides that, with a porch for bird-watching, too.

Instant vistas await users of the network—the Green Mountains over Lake Mansfield are the backdrop for the ski center.

From the center the loop begins at the gentle Sugar Road. Double tracked with a skate lane, Sugar Road is a pleasant and easy corridor through the woods. The ascent is extremely gradual, and an occasional bench welcomes rest and reflection. The cover of the woods gives way to a clearing called Picnic Knoll at the end of Sugar Road. From here you can spot Camel's Hump, wide and white, and the 4,083-foot Mount Ellen on a clear day.

The work begins at Picnic Knoll. Slayton Pasture Cabin is on the slopes of Round Top Mountain at an elevation of 2,100 feet. To get there you have to cover 700 feet of elevation gain in a couple of miles. The most popular route is the Parizo Trail. (Actually there are two Parizo Trails: One goes up; the other, down.) During the moderate climb with its few steep pitches, skiers don't have to be concerned about a smiling downhiller impeding their grunt. The trail crosses Old County Road and links up to the Cabin Trail, which rolls upward to the cabin. Stop at the cabin to rest up. That was 3 miles.

The Slayton Pasture Cabin is an ideal lunch spot for skiers and shoers in need of a break.

The Haul Road, a logging road, is a 4-mile gradual descent back to the touring center. Not too long after leaving the cabin on the Haul Road look for the jaw-dropping northern view of the alpine slopes of Smugglers' Notch and the dramatic Elephant's Head ledge. Round the trail some more and gaze east to the Worcester Range at the prominent Mount Elmore and 3,293-foot Mount Worcester. The Haul Road returns to the woods and winds down, offering a few clearings along the way. Cross Old County Road (sometimes you have to take off your skis) where 3,538-foot Hunger Mountain and Camel's Hump provide excellent vistas. Lower Haul Road links to the Luce Trail, which leads back to the ski center.

How to get there

From I–89 take exit 10 and follow Route 100 north 7.0 miles to Moscow Road. Turn left. Follow Moscow Road 1.6 miles to Barrows Road and turn right. After 2.0 miles turn left on Trapp Hill Road. Follow it 1.0 mile to the Trapp Family Lodge.

Edson Hill

Edson Hill Manor XC Touring Center, Stowe, Vermont

Type of trail:	▬ ◁ ⬤
Distance:	Nearly 4 miles
Terrain:	Hilly circuit with winter views of two mountain ranges
Trail difficulty:	More difficult
Surface quality:	Groomed for skate and classic skiers
Food and facilities:	The touring center has soups, snacks, and beverages for skiers. They offer ski and snowshoe rentals, lessons, and last-minute equipment needs. A rest room is at the center. Sleigh rides are offered and hay is often placed near the horses so skiers and snowshoers can feed them. There is a fee to use the trail system. The closest after-ski meal is in the comfort of the Edson Hill Manor, which also has fine accommodations. For those wanting to venture into Stowe, the Shed on Mountain Road (802–253–4364) brews its own beer. No dogs are allowed on the trail network.
Phone numbers:	The phone number for the Edson Hill Manor XC Touring Center is (802) 253–8954. The Edson Hill Manor can be reached at (802) 253–7371 or (800) 621–0284.

The adage what goes up must come down was never more true than at the Edson Hill Manor XC Touring Center. The 15 miles of trails have something for every level of skier, but for those wanting to exert themselves just a little, the rewards are winter views of two mountain ranges and a long, scintillating collection of downhill stretches that may leave you wondering why anyone would want to ride a high-speed quad to the top of any hill.

Snowshoers are welcome on the entire trail network, which encompasses parts of the 225-acre estate. The trails meander over meadows, up a ridge, and through the silent, peaceful forest. All of the trails are classically tracked except the upper sections, which usually aren't. Skaters may not get their fill here, but those who like to tour should. The rustic tour-

Edson Hill
Scale: 1:12,550 or 5" = 1 mile

N

START/
FINISH

Peterson

ing center sits below the manor, high on a hill. At one time the property was part of a farm-laden countryside that extended throughout the valley. Brick walls from a 1930s Burlington Hotel, fireplace tile from Holland, and Virginia brass all went into the manor. Originally built in 1940, the manor was expanded in 1954.

The touring center isn't as grand. More down-to-earth than high on a hill, the center shares the same neighborhood as the riding stables. That is part of its charm. Ski some and then feed the horses. To adults, that's romance. To a kid, that's fun.

Beginners have their trails outside the touring center where the flatter terrain is found. Trails like Bow's Field and Center Loop are where the first-timers can go. Tours in the 1- to 2-mile range can be put together using those trails.

Better skiers can try linking Old Billing Road with Maple Run for an overview of the property. The Old Billing Road is thought to be an old logging road, but some called it the "billy goat" road because it was so narrow. Maple Run passes through diverse terrain from flats to low streams and eventually along a ridge of mountains and a sugarhouse.

Three loops for more intermediate and advanced skiers can be completed individually or done together. Weave together Larry's Loop, Worcester Loop, and Sterling Run for pleasant 4-mile, two-hour journey.

The 4-mile trip results in views of moose tracks and castlelike homes, which you'll pass while tackling a steep stretch where herringbone or sidestepping skills are essential. The effort is worth it for the fast downhills and the views of frosty Mount Mansfield. Each trail has its own features. Larry's Loop was named after former Manor owner Larry Heath. The Worcester Loop has Worcester Range vistas, and Sterling Run travels to an old growth stand of birch and spruce on the edge of Sterling Ridge.

Spring Trail leads the way through a stand of pines and an open field before winding down into the woods and handing off to Larry's Loop. The climb begins immediately and does have a few forgiving spots. If the time is right, look for moose tracks by trail's edge. Sometimes the moose will tromp right across the groomed track. Up on Old Billing Road, the

Directions at a glance

0.0 Leave touring center on Spring Trail.

0.5 Turn left on Larry's Loop and make a quick right up hill.

1.0 Turn right on Old Billings Road.

1.1 Turn left on Sterling Road.

2.0 Turn right on Worcester Loop.

2.5 Turn right on Larry's Loop.

3.0 Turn right on Spring Trail and follow to touring center.

Heavy snows are held among the pines at Edson Hill Manor.

first of the hillside homes are seen. Now you see 'em through the forest, now you don't. The forest wins out and up the skier goes, pushing to the top on Sterling's Run with its three demanding pitches.

Near the top, those with energy can meander out along the Peak A View trail to a glimpse of the Stowe Valley.

The trail narrows and the pines seem big here, holding snow in their bows. No stunning views up here. Instead, the roller coaster ride begins before the mountain views come out of hibernation along Worcester Loop. There's Larry's Loop again and a passage by some homes you may wish to reside in.

Rolling and winding down, the loop is nearly complete when the touring center is seen again. Back at the center, whether you are resting by the wood stove or feeding the horses, the memories of the trail should be good.

How to get there

From Stowe Village, take Route 108 (the Mountain Road) about 3.5 miles to Edson Hill Road and turn right. Travel 1.5 miles and turn left at sign for Edson Hill Manor.

Wiessner Woods

Stowe, Vermont

Type of trail:	▬▬▬ ⬤
Also used by:	Hikers
Distance:	Nearly two miles
Terrain:	Leisurely and playful romp through the woods
Trail difficulty:	Easy
Surface quality:	Ungroomed
Food and facilities:	There are no facilities on this tour. Bring water. There are no rest rooms. Dogs are allowed. However, Stowe Village has just about everything you would need before setting out. The H. E. Shaw General Store at 207 Main Street is worth a look (802–253–4040). After the trip, the Mexican food at Miguel's on Mountain Road (802–253–7574) can spice up the day. Equipment rentals are available in Stowe. The Mountain Sports and Bike Shop on Mountain Road, by the Golden Eagle Resort, has snowshoes (802–253–7919). Umiak Outdoor Outfitters at 849 South Main Street has skis and snowshoes, too (802–253–2317).
Phone numbers:	The phone number for Stowe Land Trust is (802) 253–7221. Maps and brochures can be obtained from them by writing PO Box 274, Stowe, Vermont 05672. The Stowe Area Association on Main Street is a good resource for brochures. The number is (800) 247–8673 or (802) 253–7321.

The choices of where to ski and snowshoe in Stowe seem endless. For a fee, use the network of interconnected trails among the four touring centers in the valley. If flat is the word of the day, use the Stowe Recreation Path and create a day-long or hour-long trek.

Skiers and snowshoers wanting a leisurely romp through the forest should head to the trails of Wiessner Woods. Nothing is difficult in the woods, up above the valley. There's a bench for resting. Plentiful and colorful trail markers make navigation easy. This is where the locals ski with their dogs. It's also where tourists come bearing cameras. Add to that the Catamount Trail, and it's also a place where skiers traversing the state might be passing through.

Under the auspices of the Stowe Land Trust (SLT), the 92-acre network of trails through meadows, woods, and along streams are used for fitness and fun. If you bring a dog, it must be leashed. There is no overnight camping. Pack out what you bring in and don't stray from the

Wiessner Woods
Scale: 1:5,740 or 1" = 1 mile

START/
FINISH

trails. Follow those guidelines and the land can be enjoyed by all for years to come.

Before entering the woods there is a bench and a slab of rock with a plaque affixed to it. The plaque bears tribute to the namesake of Wiessner Woods, conservationist and mountaineer Fritz Wiessner. The Wiessner clan—Fritz, wife "Moo Moo," son Andrew, and daughter Polly—made many hikes in the woods among the abundant flora and fauna. In 1993, the tract was donated to the SLT in memory of Fritz. Now skiers and snowshoers enjoy the land that is home to deer, fox, partridge, thrush, owls, falcons, and even the occasional moose and bear. The signage, benches, and bridges within the forest are the result of donations from Stowe residents.

The SLT says that at least once a year SLT members, schoolchildren, and friends take part in a clean up day to remove fallen branches, repair winter damage, and install needed amenities.

With all this in mind, Wiessner Woods is a popular destination. Though everyone who enters the Woods from the parking area trailhead will use the Catamount Trail as the initial main thoroughfare, it is possible to branch off on several loops and not see people for long stretches at a time.

Using the trails is fairly simple. Stick to a color and follow it back to the point of origin. Green is the Sugar House Loop. Blue is the Hardwood Ridge Trail and yellow is the Meadow Trail. Frequent signs say TRAILHEAD and have an arrow pointing back to the trailhead. Actually, you are never far from the beginning.

Enter the woods on the Catamount Trail and follow it to "Four Corners." Here the loops begin.

Directions at a glance

0.0 Leave trailhead on Catamount Trail.

0.2 Turn right on Hardwood Ridge Trail.

0.5 Stay straight on Sugar House Loop.

1.3 Turn left on Hardwood Ridge Trail.

1.8 Turn left on Catamount Trail and return to trailhead parking.

Bear left and do the Meadow Loop. At right is the Hardwood Ridge Trail. A little further on is Sugar House Loop.

The Sugar House Loop is the destination here. Catamount to Hardwood Ridge to the Loop is the way to go. Travel over bridges, past tall pines, and see a Stowe snowman. The woods are an easy maze of winter paths. The sugarhouse, a place to rest a bit, borders on an abutting trail which also hosts miles of free ski and snowshoe trails. Actually, the Gameroff Sugar Shack is on that property. Feeling adventurous? Reach into the mailbox and take a map. Then explore.

For those who don't, continue on the Sugar House Loop within Wiessner Woods. If the mood strikes, create your own figure eight through the property, and enjoy the hikes done by the Wiessners.

How to get there

From Stowe Village, take Route 108 (the Mountain Road) about 3.5 miles to Edson Hill Road and turn right. Travel about .75 mile and turn right by mailbox on dirt road for Wiessner Woods (look for sign). Trailhead parking is limited.

Snowshoer meets snowman on the trails of Wiessner Woods.

Robert Frost Interpretive Trail

Ripton, Vermont

Type of trail:	
Also used by:	Hikers
Distance:	1.0 mile
Terrain:	A flat leg-stretcher or kid adventure
Trail difficulty:	Easiest
Surface quality:	Ungroomed
Food and facilities:	Pit toilet, guest book, and donation request are at the trailhead. The general store in Ripton has sandwiches for a quick post-tour bite. Nearby Middlebury has many restaurants like Green Peppers, Washington Street (802–388–3164); the Middlebury Mountaineer, 3 Mill Street (877–611–7802), rents snowshoes. The Chipman Inn, Route 125 in Ripton (802–388–2390), is near skiing.
Phone numbers:	U.S. Forest Service's Middlebury Ranger District, (802) 388–4362; Vermont State Police, (802) 244–8781.

The poet Robert Frost drank in inspiration from the woods, rivers, and mountains of Vermont and New Hampshire. Whether it be the white, supple branches of a bending birch or swift, flowing waters of a frigid river, the images found in the words of a Frost poem can be seen from the short, easy, and soothing Robert Frost Interpretive Trail.

The loop, located in the Green Mountain National Forest, is unique in that several of Frost's poems are mounted on placards along the way ("The Road not Taken," "Winter Eden," "Pasture"). Wooden benches have been placed near some of the poems as if to invite introspection. Blueberries and huckleberries at the far end of a field await new life in spring. The South Branch of the Middlebury River crosses here, and there is even a boardwalk with benches so snowshoers and skiers can pause at a frozen beaver pond. In the silence listen to the waters of the river. Not only are Frost's poems on display, but signs also indicate what types of trees are in the area, like beech, pine, birch, spruce, fir, and alder. Visitors can also learn about the wildflowers that grow here in the non-snow months.

The Forest Service uses prescribed fire to maintain the old fields and meadows along the way, preserve the scenic value of the area, and regenerate vegetation growth. The burns take place every three or four years. From the fields, Fire Tower Hill, Breadloaf Mountain, Battell

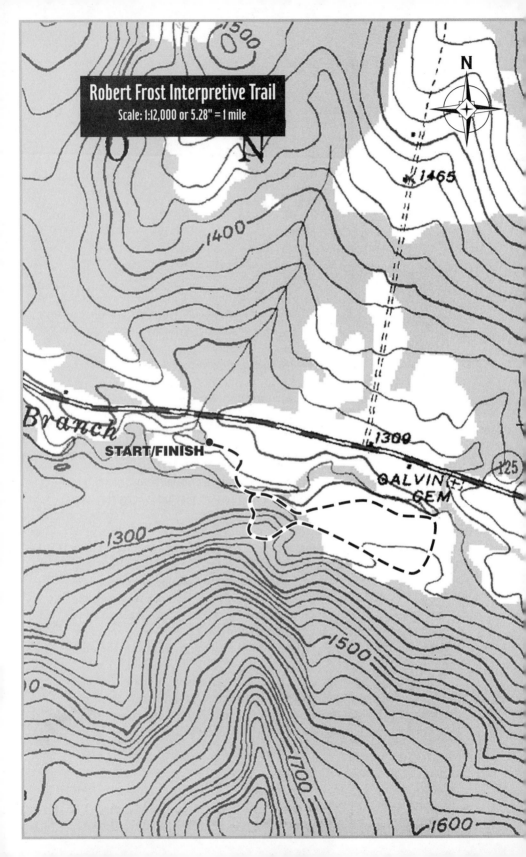

Robert Frost Interpretive Trail
Scale: 1:12,000 or 5.28" = 1 mile

N

1500

1465

1400

N

Branch

1300

START/FINISH

GALVIN
GEM

125

1300

1500

1700

1600

Mountain, Kirby Peak, and Burnt Hill provide a panorama. Frost lived in a small cabin in Ripton (about a mile from the trailhead) for twenty-three summers. Because of Frost's long association with the area (dubbed "Robert Frost Country" in 1983 by then Governor Richard Snelling), it was thought Frost's work should be commemorated. His imprint is found in many places in Vermont, from a mountain that bears his name to the stretch of Route 125 from Middlebury Gap to Hancock named Robert Frost Memorial Drive. The trail was dedicated on August 28, 1976. Frost was a Vermont poet laureate. Those not familiar with his writings might find an appreciation for them on this trail and in this setting.

Directions at a glance

0.0 Leave the trailhead, following the sign that points the way.

0.2 Bear right at arrow that says "trail."

0.3 Cross the bridge over the river and bear right, then left around the wooden bench.

0.6 Follow sign that indicates FROST TRAIL.

0.9 Bear right at sign with arrow pointing to parking.

The interpretive signs, easy terrain, benches, and views make this an ideal snowshoe for children. The signs turn the loop into a game and benches provide rest. After this loop you might enjoy this stanza from the Frost poem, "Stopping by Woods on a Snowy Evening":

> *The woods are lovely, dark, and deep,*
> *But I have promises to keep*
> *And miles to go before I sleep*
> *And miles to go before I sleep.*

How to get there

The trailhead is on Route 125 about 4 miles west of Middlebury Gap or 2 miles east of Ripton.

Maple Loop
Bolton Valley Nordic Center, Bolton Valley, Vermont

Type of trail:	▬ ◄ ▬
Distance:	3.0 miles
Terrain:	Wide, rolling romp in the shadow of Bolton Mountain
Trail difficulty:	More difficult
Surface quality:	Groomed, single track, skate
Food and facilities:	Cross-country ski and snowshoe rentals, lessons, waxing area, bathrooms, water, retail shop, snacks, and guided tours are all available at the touring center, which also doubles as the sports center with pool and sauna. Bolton Valley is an alpine ski area with slope-side hotel and condominiums. After the ski, Lori's at the Valley has that touch of casual elegance. Snowshoers are allowed on all of the trails and have some of their own too.
Phone numbers:	The general number of the Bolton Valley Resort (and hotel) is (802) 434–3444. The Nordic Center is extension 1076.

Bolton Valley is known to free-heelers for a couple of things. First, it's the starting point for one of Vermont's premier backcountry point to point skis—the Bolton-Trapp Trail. The 12-mile ungroomed adventure takes skiers over a flank on 3,840-foot Bolton Mountain and deposits them at Stowe's Trapp Family Lodge.

The Bolton-Trapp Trail isn't the only playground for three-pinners. The Bolton Valley Nordic Center has more than 60 miles of trails with only about 20 miles of them groomed. Telemark skiers can ski on the state-long Catamount Trail, other backcountry runs, or find the glades laced all over the network.

Bolton Valley is also known for its elevation. At 2,035 feet, the center lays claim to the highest elevation in the East of any cross-country ski network.

Although the snow allows the center to open from Thanksgiving to Easter and area competitive high school and college skiers use the net-

> ### Directions at a glance
>
> 0.0 Leave the touring center, via the Picnic Trail (which will become Broadway), following signs for Maple Loop.
>
> 0.6 Turn right on Maple Loop.
>
> 1.8 Turn left on Broadway and follow it back to touring center.

work to train, Bolton Valley has some of the widest trails around. About 20 miles outside Burlington, Bolton's trails average about 20 feet wide. That might bring a smile to skate skiers, but it's also good news for social skiers who tend to just schlep along. The trails have two sets of track lanes next to each other so skiers can plod along and talk side by side.

Also, skiers with dogs will find their own 8-mile network of trails called Doggie World. Located on the lower part of the mountain, away from the touring center, these trails give pet owners the chance to ski with their canines without having to endure the stares of nondog people on skis.

The cross-country ski area, adjacent to the twin-peaked downhill ski area, began in the late 1960s when founder Gardiner Lane took existing logging roads and began cutting them into ski trails. Upkeep of the cross-

The downhill ski trails at Bolton Valley can be seen from the cross-country network.

country area has fluctuated over the years, but there's been a recent effort to put some muscle and money into the cross-country ski trails. More trails could surface in the future, as well as night skiing.

Advanced skiers like the sinuous World Cup circuit, which pumps up that heart rate through a climb into the woods easily seen from the touring center. Closer to the touring center is the beginner Picnic Loop where first timers usually make their first tracks. Snowshoers can do the Valley Loop for views to the Adirondacks, while Pond Loop skims the frozen waters near the touring center.

Signs of wildlife are scattered throughout the network. Eagle-eyed skiers might see signs of moose, the claw marks left by bears reaching up trees, or a vacant bird's nest.

Intermediate skiers can take a tour on the wide side by combining Broadway and Maple Loop. Broadway is a long connector trail that bisects the network. The name refers to its broad width, not to theaters found along its way. The trail parallels a brook and is the path used to get to Maple Loop. Though the circuit can be done either way, doing it counterclockwise ensures the skier of some rollicking downhills on Maple Loop.

The loop briefly utilizes the Picnic Loop near the snow-covered tennis courts and past trailside condos before joining Broadway and crossing Joiner Brook on a bridge. Though there aren't any maps saying "you are here" along the route, the rustic signs are ample. Climb Maple Loop gradually and enjoy the hairpin and S-turns just after the junction with Spruce Run (a bailout for those who tire easily). The twisting downhill is exhilarating. Bolton Valley's Ricker and Vista Peaks are easily seen through the trees. On Broadway, spotted with slabs of ice-gripped rock, the mountain ridgeline is an in-your-face view for much of the uphill back to the touring center.

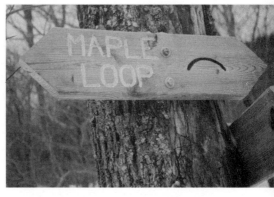

The Maple Loop is part of the trail system at Bolton Valley.

How to get there

From I–89, take either exit 10 or exit 11. Follow Route 2 for 8 miles and turn onto the Bolton Valley Access Road. The touring center is 4 miles up the sometimes steep road.

Camel's Hump View Trail

Camel's Hump State Park, Waterbury, Vermont

Type of trail:	━━━ ⬭
Also used by:	Hikers
Distance:	Nearly 1.0 mile
Terrain:	Excellent views for minimal effort
Trail difficulty:	Easiest
Surface quality:	Ungroomed, skier packed
Food and facilities:	There are no facilities at the trailhead. For food Waterbury has a Grand Union on Main Street, or try Arvads (802–244–8973), also on Main Street. Lodging is available at The Cedars Inn, 129 Maple Street, Waterbury Center (802–244–7486). Rentals are in nearby Stowe.
Phone numbers:	Vermont State Department of Forests, Parks and Recreation Office, Waterbury, (802) 241–3678 for more information.

It is not too often the word *easy* is used in conjunction with Camel's Hump. Vermont's hunchback of winter, the 4,063-foot-high peak is one of the state's most prominent features and is also a summit devoid of any development, like ski lifts or antennas. From the gentle and welcoming Camel's Hump View Trail, skiers and snowshoers can pause on a bench and take in the views of the mountain a few miles away.

Camel's Hump View is a relatively new wheelchair-accessible path built in the early 1990s. Because it must accommodate wheelchairs during the nonsnow months, it is wide and its grade is gentle. This 0.8-mile loop is a very easy excursion, ideal for the family. The kids will enjoy trying to ski or snowshoe from bench to bench, crossing a bridge, looking for the work done by woodpeckers, or trying to identify the animal tracks—like those of a snowshoe hare—in the snow. The benches are also good spots for a lunch.

Camel's Hump State Park is in the northern half of Vermont's Green Mountains. The park had its beginnings in 1911 when a man named Colonel Joseph Battell of Middlebury donated 1,000 acres of land, including the summit of Camel's Hump, to preserve the view from his home. Since then the park has grown to about 24,000 acres.

The Camel's Hump View Trail begins at a well-marked trailhead. The loop can be done in either direction, but we'll go counterclockwise to enjoy the downhill near the end of the loop. Blue blazes mark the way as the trail begins by the rushing waters of Sinnott Brook. It's not too long before you reach the first bench. Stop to admire the view of Camel's Hump off in the distance. Near the midway mark Camel's Hump View intersects with the Ridley Crossing Cross-Country Ski Trail. A possible side trip for better skiers, the ski trail, marked with blue diamonds, is sandwiched between Ridley and Sinnott Brooks. At 0.9 miles it reaches the Beaver Meadow Trail, a section of the Vermont Association of Snow Travelers network of snowmobile trails. (One can either return to Camel's Hump View, or, by turning right on Beaver Meadow, go on for more than a mile

Directions at a glance

0.0 Leave the trailhead and follow the blue-blazed Camel's Hump View Trail.

0.3 The Ridley Crossing Cross-Country Ski Trail enters right. Continue to the left, following the blue blazes around and back to the trailhead.

before coming back to Camel's Hump Road, where a right turn and a short walk bring you back to the Camel's Hump View Trailhead.)

On Camel's Hump View the trail snakes near Sinnott Brook and then begins to head down on the other side of the brook. More benches mark

the way. You see Camel's Hump through the evergreens as the trail descends and banks to the left. The familiar parking lot is soon ahead, but first head over the bridge built by the On Top School in 1993. There is a final bench here before you reach the parking lot.

How to get there

From I–89 take exit 10. Travel on Route 2 east 0.1 mile and make a right on Winooski Street. Travel about 0.5 mile and cross over a bridge. Turn right after the bridge. This is Duxbury Road. Follow it 4.0 miles and make a left on Camel's Hump Road. The trailhead is about 3.5 miles down the road.

Burrows Trail

Camel's Hump State Park, Huntington Center, Vermont

Type of trail:	(icon)
Also used by:	Backcountry skiers, hikers
Distance:	4.8 miles round-trip
Terrain:	Hilly trek above treeline for experienced snowshoers
Trail difficulty:	Most difficult
Surface quality:	Ungroomed, but packed
Food and facilities:	There are no facilities at the trailhead. Jaque's Country Store and Deli (802–434–2674) in Huntington, on Main Road, is for last minute items and the post-trip sandwich; later consider the buffet at the House of Tang on River Street, Montpelier (802–223–6020). The state capital has plentiful lodging offerings like the Econolodge (800–553–2666). Onion River Sports on Lincoln Street in Montpelier has rentals (802–229–9409).
Phone numbers:	Call the Essex Junction office of the Vermont State Department of Forests, Parks and Recreation (802–879–6565) or the department headquarters in Waterbury (802–241–3678) for information.

The Green Mountain Club estimates some 20,000 people ascend to the top of Camel's Hump each year. The hike to its 4,083-foot summit is popular in summer, and snowshoeing and skiing on the mountain have been gaining momentum during winter. Ascending Camel's Hump is a trip that should be well planned and done with caution. Clear skies and calm winds can change immediately to 40-mile-per-hour gusts and

The Burrows Trail waits for fresh tracks on the way up or down Camel's Hump.

whiteout conditions. Knowing the forecast is of prime importance.

On Camel's Hump the winter enthusiast is above the treeline and exposed to wind. Icy and windswept conditions can haunt a summit, and the open ridges make snowshoes impractical. Crampons are better.

Backcountry skiers can combine skiing and snowshoeing on this one. Many favor the section of the Burrows Trail featured in this trip as a skin-up, ski-down experience.

The summit of the double-humped mountain in Camel's Hump State Park supports Arctic-alpine vegetation. Many of the plants are on the state's endangered species list. Travel only on the marked trails to protect the fragile ecosystem. Though winter sometimes hangs on in Vermont, and snow might still be found at higher elevations, the trails to Camel's Hump usually are closed by mid-April for a few weeks to minimize damage during spring meltdown. Heed this rule.

The blue-blazed Burrows Trail, which leaves from a plowed dirt parking area, scales the western side of the mountain. Enter the woods and proceed to the signboard where winter recreationists are encouraged to sign in. The trailhead is also a starting point for another way up the mountain. Though longer, it is possible to snowshoe up to the summit by taking the Burrows–Forest City Connector Trail for 0.1 mile to a left on the Forest City Trail to Wind Gap, where a left on the Long Trail heads up to the summit.

The Burrows Trail is initially wide and is a moderate climb in the beginning, passing a bench with a view looking down on a rushing stream.

As the trail progresses it narrows as groves of evergreen trees enter the landscape. The Burrows Trail will

> ### Directions at a glance
>
> 0.0 Leave to the right of the signboard on the Burrows Trail.
>
> 2.1 Turn right at junction and travel 0.3 to the summit.
>
> Return via the same route.

also get progressively steeper until it reaches a clearing some 0.3 mile from the summit. The flat clearing is a spot where many trails intersect.

Turning right leads to the treeless, rocky summit.

The summit is a stunning, unspoiled area. From it New Hampshire's White Mountains lie to the east. Vermont's Green Mountains spread along a north-south corridor. The Adirondacks in New York appear in the western sky.

From here descend along the same route some 2,000 feet back to the trailhead.

How to get there

From I–89 take exit 11 and then Route 2 east to Richmond. Turn left on Bridge Street and follow it to Huntington Center. Turn left on Camel's Hump Road and follow the road 3.5 miles to the trailhead. Four-wheel drive is suggested for the last mile. If not available, park by the lower unplowed trailhead and walk 0.7 mile to the winter trailhead.

Faulkner Trail
Woodstock, Vermont

Type of trail:	(symbol)
Also used by:	Hikers
Distance:	1.6 miles one way, 3.2 miles round-trip
Terrain:	Fine, hilly in-town excursion with out-of-town vistas
Trail difficulty:	Easiest, except for the last 0.1 mile, which is steep and rocky
Surface quality:	Ungroomed
Food and facilities:	There are no facilities. In Woodstock there is a Grand Union on Route 4. After the trip try the Fireside Lounge for lunches and picnics to go, South Street (802–457–6672). Skiers wishing to access the summit of Mount Tom can do so via the Sleigh Ride Trail groomed and maintained by the Woodstock Ski Touring Center. That trail is 2.0 miles each way. Snowshoers are also welcome on the Sleigh Ride Trail. There is an access fee for that trail. Rentals are available at the touring center. The Woodstock Inn (802–448–7900) is a rewarding place to stay.
Phone numbers:	Woodstock Ski Touring Center, (802) 457–6674. (The center offers an extensive network of mapped and marked trails that are immediately adjacent. The center itself is located a half mile south of the village green on Route 106.)

Faulkner Trail
Scale: 1:12,000 or 5.28" = 1 mile

N

PATH

1000

888

Mt Tom

300

701

River Street
Cem

697

700

START/FINISH

Faulkner
Park

900

900

800

From the summit of Mount Tom in Woodstock, the views of Vermont are stunning.

The top of Mount Tom's south peak in winter offers a splendid panorama of central Vermont and the upper Connecticut River Valley into New Hampshire. Even from a wooden semicircular bench by Woodstock's illuminating Christmas star, you can see the quaintness that is Woodstock. Mountains, hills, and neat farms are off in the distance. Down below, like a miniature town from a childhood railroad display, Woodstock is alive. Smoke rises from the woodstoves and fireplaces. The Ottauquechee River cuts its path through town. The Federal-style, immaculate homes that line the village green appear diminutive. Even the covered bridge in town is visible. The mountain top offers a clear glimpse into the way Rockefeller money has preserved both history and land in Woodstock.

Directions at a glance

0.0 Leave Mountain Avenue on the unsigned Faulkner Trail by the stone wall at one end of Faulkner Park and enter the woods. Follow the yellow-blazed trail to the left.

1.2 Turn left on the Faulkner Trail (there's a sign). The Link Trail enters from the right.

1.5 Bench with an open view.

1.6 Top of Mount Tom's south peak.

Return the same way.

To snowshoe up 1,240-foot Mount Tom in winter is to have an Old World experience. The yellow-blazed Faulkner Trail is a series of switchbacks that zigzag up to the top where an old carriage road loops around. Follow the circular path and be treated to views of the village, Killington Peak, Mount Ascutney, Mount Peg, and the mountains of the Granite State. The grade up the Faulkner Trail is very gentle, and the many benches placed along the way, though some may be covered with snow, are places to rest. Huge boulders, left behind as the glaciers retreated, call the mountain home. In winter ice clings to the stones with chilling fingers. Stone walls reach out from the snow, and a stone bridge is nearby.

Faulkner Park on Mountain Avenue is obvious but not signed. The unmarked trail begins by a stone wall next to a stunning white home with pond, gazebo, and picnic table. The trail enters the woods by a huge rock, bears left, and immediately begins the switchbacks that make the trail so easy to follow. Though obvious shortcuts present themselves, it is best to stick to the trail. At least on the way up.

After about 1.0 mile the Link Trail enters right by an old railing, and the Faulkner Trail bears to the left. The trail passes large rock faces and the views through the trees are impressive. A wooden bench on a knoll offering vistas of the village and hills marks the 1.5-mile mark.

The next 100 yards to the summit of the south peak is not an easy jaunt. The trail drops quickly and then climbs steeply and narrowly over rocks. A handrail is there for assistance. At the top be sure to head around the carriage road. In winter the Woodstock Ski Touring Center grooms the carriage road as part of its 35 miles of trails. Be courteous and don't snowshoe on the groomed tracks. There is plenty of room for everyone.

To return to the park, return the same way, following the sign that reads MOUNTAIN AVENUE. Carefully descend the path back to the wooden bench. Once there let the fun begin. Use your discretion in romping through the snow on the way back down.

How to get there

Faulkner Park is located on Mountain Avenue in Woodstock. There are a number of parking alternatives in winter. Park across the street from the Woodstock Recreation Department in the parking area on Route 4. Walk to the park by turning left on Mountain Avenue to Faulkner Park.

Hogback Trail

Blueberry Hill Nordic Center, Goshen, Vermont

Type of trail:	▬▬ ◄ ⬤
Distance:	3.8 miles
Terrain:	Hilly and exciting romp through the woods
Trail difficulty:	More difficult
Surface quality:	Groomed, single tracked, skate lane
Food and facilities:	Rentals (skis and snowshoes), lessons, a wax room, retail shop, and cafe are located at the Blueberry Hill Nordic Center. There is a trail fee to use the network. Lodging and dinner are available at the Blueberry Hill Inn. Reservations are requested.
Phone numbers:	Blueberry Hill Nordic Center and Inn, (802) 247–6735 or (800) 448–0707.

Vermont's Green Mountain National Forest is divided in two, with northern and southern sections. The 20,000 acres that make up the northern part, called Moosalamoo, is home to more than 60 miles of groomed cross-country ski trails maintained by the Blueberry Inn, Rikert Ski Touring Center, and Churchill House Inn, as well as the Catamount Trail and other systems.

The Blueberry Hill Nordic Center is run by one of Vermont's skiing pioneers, Tony Clark. A Brit who grew up in France skiing in the heights of the Alps, this ski mountaineer moved to the area in 1967. At the suggestion of a friend, Johannes Von Trapp, Clark and his then wife opened the center in 1971. The Nordic Center was a ramshackle operation initially, operating on donations. Since then it has grown to encompass 40 miles of trails (snowshoers are welcome on the network) and is home to a resplendent inn as well. To help skiers and snowshoers get around, trails east of the inn are odd-numbered, and trails to the west are even-numbered. The inn is number one, so if someone loses the way, all they have to do is follow the numbers in descending order back to the center.

Clark has a vision. His legacy is to turn the trail network into a non-profit foundation and open the system to the public on a no-fee basis, totally supported by Moosalamoo Partnership.

The loop begins with a gentle dip behind the blue inn, which was built in 1813, crossing a brook and then heading upward through the woods. The trail system is constructed in such a way that there are a series of climbs with plateaus, offering a flat respite as a reward for every effort.

START/FINISH

Hogback Trail
Scale: 1:24,000 or 2.64" = 1 mile

The quaint Blueberry Hill Inn is across the road from the touring center.

The Hogback Trail undergoes a name change and becomes the Zach Osborne Trail after about 0.3 mile. Osborne ran the ski center during the 1994–95 season and worked long, hard hours maintaining the trail he loved. In January 1997, at the age of 39, he died of cancer. The trail was named in his honor.

The trail undulates through land that was once part of the farms in the area. At about midway through the loop, you reach one of the most stunning vistas in the state as the mountains swell in the distance. Leave the shelter of the woods and come out to a clearing where to the west lie the Adirondacks, the Taconics to the south, and the Green Mountains and the Long Trail to the east. The hump that is Hogback rises up like a 2,286-foot-high hunchback. Pause before twisting down for a return to the woods.

Directions at a glance

0.0   Leave on the Hogback Trail, which begins behind the inn.

0.3   Turn right at junction 7 where the trail becomes the Zach Osborne Trail.

0.8   Bear left at junction 21.

2.1   Turn left at junction 25.

3.2   Turn left on the Lee Todd Trail at junction 29; follow the trail 0.6 mile back to the inn.

After the vista the Halfdan Kuhnle Trail leaves right for a 2.5-mile climb up Romance Mountain. For expert skiers the path is the highest groomed trail in the state. The

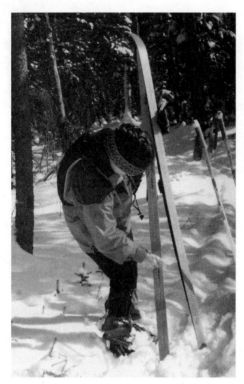

loop continues left with a change of vegetation. Now that they are on the east side of the mountain, skiers follow a ridge that overlooks a gully in the spruce and softwood forest.

The trail comes to a junction, number 29, and swings left on the Lee Todd Trail, named after a former ski center director, and finishes back to the inn on a gorgeous downhill.

How to get there

From Brandon follow Route 73 east 4 miles to Forest Road 32. Turn left. Drive 4 miles to the Blueberry Hill Nordic Center.

Waxable skis will make a trek more enjoyable because snow conditions change with the weather and the thermometer.

South Ridge Loop

Mountain Meadows Cross-Country Ski Center, Killington, Vermont

Type of trail:	▬▬ ◄
Distance:	5.4 miles
Terrain:	A few steeps, but an exhilarating ride
Trail difficulty:	Most difficult
Surface quality:	Groomed, single tracked, skate lane
Food and facilities:	Rentals (skis and snowshoes), a wax room, lessons, retail shop, and snack bar are available at Mountain Meadows. The Killington après-ski scene is legendary. The Wobbly Barn rocks (802–422–6171). For lodging, call Killington at (800) 621–MTNS.
Phone numbers:	Mountain Meadows, (800) 221–0598.

Make sure your seatbelts are fastened for a ride on the South Ridge Loop at Mountain Meadows Cross-Country Ski Center in central Vermont. The undulating trail, which opened in December 1997, dances up, down, and around through the woods, by rounded mountains, and past huge boulders and includes a half-mile downhill with exhilarating hairpin turns. Though the trail is virtually new, it has quickly become a favorite among more advanced skiers and may also evolve into the network's banner run.

At one time the area that is Mountain Meadows was a working farm with cattle, sheep, and apple orchards. Though there are still remnants of those days—home foundations and stone walls throughout the northern section of the network—the 37 miles of groomed trails are now within sight of the alpine slopes of Killington and Pico. Snowshoers are not allowed on the ski trails but have their own 6 miles of trails to explore.

Unique to Mountain Meadows is a color-coded trail system. The entire network is composed of loops. Instead of having trail signs with numbers or names, the signs are color coded. Want to do a loop? Just follow its color. Borrowing an idea from our Canadian neighbors, Mountain Meadows also posts distances in descending order back to the touring center. As a loop progresses, the distance is posted at one kilometer intervals, so skiers know how far it is back to the center. These two elements save skiers from having to think too much.

The ski begins with an easy downhill to the frozen shores of Kent Pond (also known as Kent Lake), which is rimmed by hills. Ski over a small portion of the lakeshore before entering the woods and traversing rolling terrain. A short climb of about 100 vertical feet eventually flattens

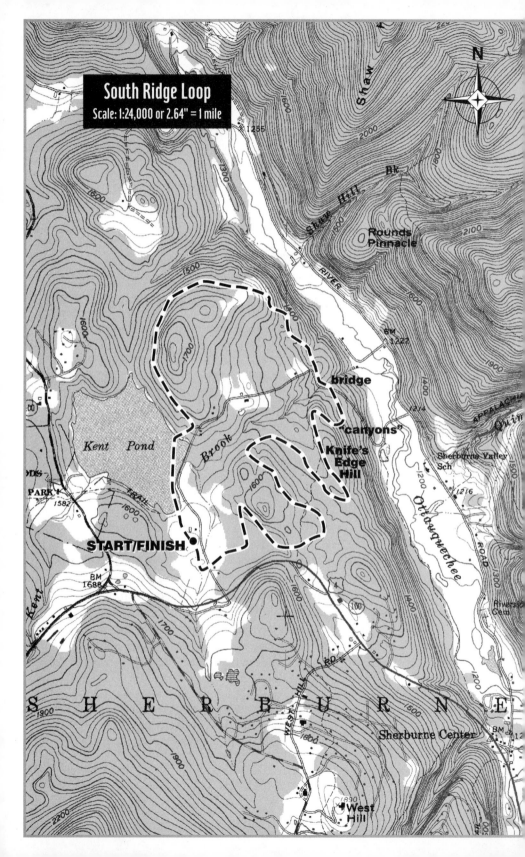

South Ridge Loop
Scale: 1:24,000 or 2.64" = 1 mile

N

Shaw Hill Bk

Rounds
Pinnacle

RIVER

BM
1227

bridge

"canyons"

Knife's
Edge
Hill

Sherburne Valley
Sch

1216

Kent   Pond

Brook

Ottauquechee

APPALACHIAN

Quin

ROAD

Riverside
Cem

DS
PARK

1582

TRAIL

1600

START/FINISH

BM
1688

100

Kent

1700

RD

WEST HILL RO

Sherburne Center

BM

S H E R B U R N E

1900

1900

West
Hill

out and leads skiers to a picnic table, covered in snow in winter. Here the roller coaster ride begins. Mountain Meadows doesn't pull punches about its terrain. Signs warn skiers that if they aren't confident on their boards, don't try it. The rip-roaring descent twists and turns through the old apple orchards. The rounded peaks of the River Road Valley serve as a backdrop seen through the trees.

The long downhill ends by crossing Thundering Brook Road where it's a fifty-fifty shot whether you should take off your skis. The trail picks up on the other side of the road and parallels the pristine Thundering Brook for a short spell. (Though they aren't seen on this ski, the falls upstream are the second highest in the state.)

Up and down, like the huge swells of a stormy sea, the trail moves through the forest in a series of switchbacks. Some sections are rather steep, like an area dubbed the "Canyon" because of its resemblance to one. Another hill sure to make skiers use the herringbone technique is the one named "Knife's Edge," which takes skiers up on a razorback under a tall pine grove.

A sweeping turn brings skiers out into a marsh with cattails poking through the snow and the ski slopes up ahead. The touring center is in sight, and it's only a short distance back to it.

Directions at a glance

0.0 Leave from behind the touring center on the South Ridge Trail or brown loop.

0.5 Turn right at the brown-colored sign.

0.6 Turn left at the brown-colored sign marked E.

1.8 Bear left at the brown-colored sign marked L.

2.5 Cross Thundering Brook Road and pick up the trail on the other side.

5.2 Cross Thundering Brook Road and pick up the trail for 0.2 mile back to the touring center.

How to get there

From the intersection of Routes 100 and 4 in Killington, follow Route 4 one-quarter mile east past the access road to Killington. Turn left on Thundering Brook Road to Mountain Meadows.

Lost Horizon Loop

Mountain Top Inn Cross-Country Ski Resort, Chittendon, Vermont

Type of trail: ▬▬ ◄ ▩

Distance: 8.5 miles

Terrain: Challenging mountain circuit by the spine of the Green Mountains

Trail difficulty: Most difficult

Surface quality: Tracked, skate groomed

Food and facilities: Rentals, lessons, snack bar, wax hut, and retail shop specializing in racing are all found at the Mountain Top Inn Cross-Country Ski Resort. Pamper yourself by staying at the Mountain Top Inn or dining in the restaurant after the ski.

Phone numbers: For the cross-country center, (802) 483–6089. The Mountain Top Inn and the restaurant can be reached at (800) 445–2100 or (802) 483–2311.

The Mountain Top Inn gets high ratings from the cross-country community for its plentiful and challenging terrain. But first, let's get something straight: This isn't golf course skiing. If flat is what you want, go elsewhere.

However, if looking down on the Chittendon Reservoir after making a long haul through a forever-changing forest is your idea of fun, then Mountain Top is the right place. The reservoir is at 1,495 feet while the mountaintop stands at 2,174 feet.

Skiers and snowshoers are welcome on the more than 50 miles of groomed trails of the 1,000-acre resort that abuts private lands and Green Mountain National Forest. At more than 2,000 feet in elevation, the resort operates from December to mid-March, attracting area race teams and experienced Nordic skiers.

> ## Directions at a glance
>
> 0.0 Leave the touring center on Interfield.
>
> 0.25 Turn left on Loggerhead.
>
> 1.0 Go straight on Sunset.
>
> 2.0 Straight on Red Alert.
>
> 2.3 Turn left on Lost Horizon.
>
> 6.0 Turn left on Boondocks.
>
> 7.0 Turn right on Hewitt Brook back to touring center.

"There's generally a ten degree difference in temperature between here and Rutland 12 miles away," says longtime trail manager Don Cochrane.

Lost Horizon Loop
Scale: 1:14,000 or 4.25" = 1 mile

Just to be sure, Mountain Top has a small amount of snowmaking on portions of trails like Morning Glory, Turkey Track, Loggerhead, and Lower Interfield.

Cochrane has been here since 1973, longer than present inn owners Mike and Maggie Gehan who recently bought the charming mountainside property. Established in 1945, the inn saw a visit from President Eisenhower in the 1950s and was rebuilt in 1977 after a fire. Not far from the peaks of Killington, the center attracts lots of day-trippers and its share of inn guests.

One of the most popular runs is the 1.5-mile-long Deer Run from near the summit. The rolling wooded run is known for its four-legged visitors. Though the parking lot can be full, the area disperses skiers easily and there is quiet in the hardwood forest on runs like Bonny Lass and Round Robin. Round Robin is adventurous. It is a 12-mile ski around the lake. Skiers aren't allowed to attempt the loop past 11:00 A.M. Experts can try Nosedive, a 0.5-mile run from the summit.

Lost Horizon is a 3.6-mile trail, one of the longest at the resort, that bobs up and down the mountain. It's the showcase in a loop that isn't too arduous but has some heart-pumping ups and downs. The circuit begins by leaving the renovated horse barn (known as the touring center) and skiing an easy portion of Upper Interfield past the snowmaking pond before a steep haul up Loggerhead with a viewpoint down to the reservoir. Sunset has winter views to the west of the Adirondacks while Red Alert is a downhill blast to the weaving Lost Horizon that ventures into the Green Mountain National Forest. Ride the roller coaster to Boondocks and into the hardwoods. Then it's uphill on Hewitt Brook back to the touring center and the warming woodstove.

How to get there

Turn left from Route 4/100 onto Meadowlake Drive, right on Chittendon Road, and left on Mountain Top Road to the Mountain Top Inn. For the cross-country center, turn left on Mountain Spring Road past the inn. The route is well signed.

Merck Forest and Farmland Center's Birch Pond Loop

Rupert, Vermont

Type of trail:	▬▬ ▰
Also used by:	Hikers
Distance:	3.5 miles
Terrain:	A flat to hilly winter adventure unlike any other
Trail difficulty:	Easiest
Surface quality:	Ungroomed, but skier tracked
Food and facilities:	Pop in to the Joy Green Visitor Center at the Merck Forest and Farmland Center before heading out. There are rest rooms, water, and snacks. Cabins are available for overnight use for a fee. Nearby Manchester has everything you want in terms of groceries, rentals, and restaurants. In Manchester try Candeleros on Main Street for Mexican food, (802) 362–0836. Cross-country ski and snowshoe rentals are at the Mountain Goat, Route 7A (Historic Main Street) in Manchester, (802) 362–5159.
Phone numbers:	Merck Forest and Farmland Center, (802) 394–7836; Rupert Police, (802) 394–7778.

Ski by a wide, open field with views of the hills of New York and stop to watch horses eat some hay. Snowshoe by a handsome farm and watch the cattle eating. Enter into a maple grove and see the taps in the trees for the collection of sap, which will be boiled down into syrup.

These and other experiences await visitors to the Merck Forest and Farmland Center in southern Vermont. (As employees are quick to note, the center is not affiliated with the Merck Company.) Located on 3,150 acres of hilltop working farm and forest land, the center is an environmental educational organization in the Taconic Range. Recreational and educational programs abound on its 28 miles of snowshoe and cross-country ski trails.

This nonprofit organization looks to the community for support, and it welcomes memberships and donations. There is no charge to use the trails. In winter romp through the snow-covered fields and forests. Programs range from mammal tracking to snowshoe making. Full-moon snowshoeing, and a maple-sugaring celebration are also offered during winter. Or spend a day indoors learning how to make a packbasket while other family members head out on the trails. Nature displays can be found at the visitor center and in the farmhouse on Old Town Road.

It is fairly easy to get around the property. Its signs are easy to read

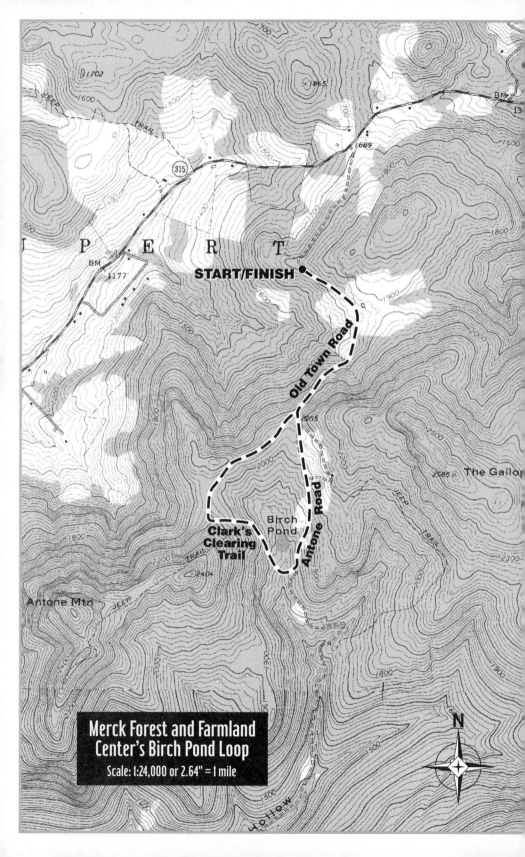

START/FINISH

Old Town Road

Antone Road

Birch Pond

Clark's Clearing Trail

Antone Mtn

The Gallop

Merck Forest and Farmland Center's Birch Pond Loop

Scale: 1:24,000 or 2.64" = 1 mile

N

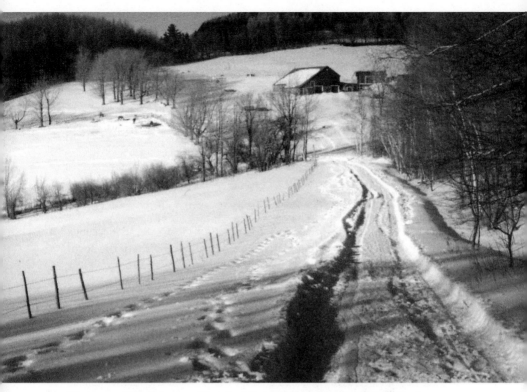

The beauty of Merck Forest and Farmland Center is reflected on the Old Town Road.

though they do not have distances on them. The trails are not marked with occasional blazes or markers as in national forests, which is a slight drawback. This might prove worrisome to those new to the outdoor experience. If that is the case, just ask at the visitor center for the trails that have seen recent usage. These packed paths will be easy to follow.

We've put together an interesting 3.5-mile loop to give visitors a taste of what is on the property. But feel free to explore a side trail, particularly after a fresh snow.

Old Town Road is a wide, unplowed road that goes through the heart of the property. Remember this is a working farm. Wide, thick wheels from farm equipment provide a country track for skiers. Or you can ski or snowshoe on the bank of snow left between the tires. Leave the visitor center on Old Town Road as it opens up to a stunning vista of farm, hills, and horses. A cabin and barn appear on the right. The barn appears more like a castle in the winter's outdoor beauty. Pass by the horses, then turn right with Old Town Road as it climbs steadily along. Enjoy the stunning views of the Taconics. On both sides several trails leave Old Town Road. At the height of the land, a road to a lodge diverges left and one to Mount Antone leaves right. Continue straight on Old Town.

Admire the stands of spruce and hilltops. Old Town Road descends quickly here as it passes along a maple grove. In late February the sugar maple trees are tapped with a line that stretches from tree to tree. Near the 1.5-mile mark, a sign points to Birch Pond. As an excellent diversion you can return along the same way. To make the loop turn right by the sign to Birch Pond, a small pond set among the hills.

Clark's Clearing Trail ascends the forested hill. There won't be a sign yet. There is one for Schenk Road, which leads to Clark's Clearing Trail. The trail has a few steep grades as it climbs upward along the flanks of Mount Antone. The trail reaches a small cabin called the Clark's Clearing Cabin. (In the cabin are a bunk bed, table, and woodstove.) A number of trails intersect here. Just turn right at the cabin for Antone Road and head to the clearing for a beautiful vista. Antone Road slopes downward to join up with Old Town Road. Bear left on Old Town Road (this junction should look familiar) and follow it back down to the visitor center.

How to get there

From Manchester travel on West Road 3.5 miles. Turn left on Route 30 north to Dorset. Travel 5.5 miles and turn left on Route 315. Go about 3.0 miles and turn left at the Merck Forest and Farmland Center in Rupert.

Little Michigan/Stone Place Trails Loop

Landgrove, Vermont

Type of trail:	▬▬▬ ⬭
Also used by:	Small portion by snowmobilers
Distance:	4.0 miles
Terrain:	Hilly workout along a part of the Catamount Ski Trail
Trail difficulty:	More and most difficult
Surface quality:	Ungroomed, skier tracked
Food and facilities:	There are no facilities available on this loop. Cross-country ski and snowshoe rentals and lessons can be had at the Landgrove Inn, Little Michigan Road, Landgrove (802–824–6673), a short distance from the trailhead. The West River Nordic Ski Club's Trail Network with a few miles of groomed trails is at the inn. It has some beginners' trails. Donations are accepted. For groceries try the Mountain Marketplace shopping center at the junctions of Routes 11 and 100 in Londonderry. Jake's Cafe (802–824–6614) is there for a post-ski meal. The Landgrove Inn serves dinner Thursday through Sunday evenings.
Phone numbers:	Green Mountain National Forest Manchester Ranger District, (802) 362–2307; Mountain Valley Trails Association, (802) 824–4166.

Skiers and snowshoers looking for a 10-mile network of challenging trails in southern Vermont should head to the rural village of Landgrove and the Mountain Valley Trails Association area in the Green Mountain National Forest. The farms, brooks, horses, old cemeteries, and New England quaintness are a most pleasant diversion from the intermediate and advanced trails on the surrounding hills.

Located in the national forest, the trails are ungroomed and open to the public at no charge. (There are a few loop options available, like the 7.0-mile Little Michigan Loop.) They are well marked with blue diamonds and signs. Here, we go a little more than half that distance in a hillside workout that also encompasses Vermont's legendary Catamount Cross-Country Ski Trail.

Snowmobilers like this part of the world, too. You share the trail, Forest Road 10, with them for only a short distance.

The Little Michigan Loop trailhead is on Forest Road 10. Ski on the wide forest road beyond the sign board to a sign that points left to the Catamount Ski Trail/Utley Brook Trail. A black diamond ski sign indicates that the route is most difficult. That may well be because of the climb involved. In reality, initially, the Utley Brook Trail wiggles through the evergreens like a playful puppy. But that puppy grows up rather quickly and takes a snap at you from time to time with a few heart-stopping pitches and narrow slots through the trees.

Remember that some of the trails in the Green Mountain National Forest go through periods of active timber operations, so don't be surprised if you run into one from time to time. The trail widens considerably as it passes through the harvest area up along the side of a hill. The reward is a hoot of a ski down to the junction with the Little Michigan Trail. Turn left on Little Michigan for a short and gentle climb to the junction with the Stone Place Trail. Skiers and shoers looking for the 7.0-mile loop should continue on the Little Michigan Trail until reaching the Jones Brook Trail and returning to the parking area.

Turn left for the Stone Place Trail and descend. The trail includes a small section that is a wide, flat unplowed country road. Ski down and at the junction with the road, turn right. Enjoy the flatness and brightness. At about 0.2 mile a bridge off to the left crosses picturesque Griffith Brook. Cross the railed bridge as the trail continues a moderate climb. The trail plays with the sun: Sometimes it is sunny in spots; other times, shaded by the forest pines.

Directions at a glance

0.0 From the Little Michigan trailhead on Forest Road 10, ski down the road a few yards until reaching a sign for the Catamount Cross-Country Ski Trail. Turn left. This is the Utley Brook Trail.

1.2 Turn left on Little Michigan Trail.

1.4 Turn left on Stone Place Trail.

1.5 Turn right on the Stone Place Trail.

1.7 Turn left over the bridge on the Stone Place Trail.

2.4 Turn left on the Jones Brook Trail.

3.7 Turn left on groomed trail, part of West River Nordic Ski Club system. It is unsigned. Continue straight for a few yards. Trail will bear right. Ski down hill to the left into meadow and continue bearing left to ski club parking area on Little Michigan Road. Turn left out of parking area on Little Michigan Road.

3.8 Turn right on Forest Road 10.

4.0 To the left is the Little Michigan trailhead.

A junction marks a left turn onto the Jones Brook Trail. Like a winter desert, small young growths poke through the snow. The distant alpine slopes of Bromley act as a backdrop. The Jones Brook Trail rolls downward before darting left back into the woods. Over the next 1.0 mile, the trail has several rolling hills, including an exhilarating sweeping hairpin curve.

The Jones Brook Trail comes to a T junction with a groomed trail, part of the West River Nordic Ski Club's Trail Network. Turn left on the velvetlike thoroughfare and ski a few yards. The trail will bear right. Instead, shoot down that hill to the left and into the meadow. Continue bearing left until you reach the ski club's parking area.

From here either ski back to the car by turning left on Little Michigan Road and right on FR 10, or take off the skis, watch the horses, and stretch those legs before walking back to the car.

How to get there

From the junction of Routes 100 and 11 in Londonderry, travel on Route 11 west. Proceed 0.5 mile and turn right on Landgrove Road. Follow Landgrove Road 4.2 miles and turn left on Little Michigan Road. One-half mile later, turn right on Forest Road 10. A sign will point to Danby. The trailhead is 0.2 mile down on the left, but parking is not allowed there because it is a plow turnaround point. Park along the road but not in front of the NO PARKING signs.

Not exactly Detroit. A skier digs into his backpack along the Little Michigan Trail.

Grout Pond Loop Trail

Stratton, Vermont

Type of trail: ▬▬▬ ⬬

Also used by: Portion by snowmobilers

Distance: 4.8 miles

Terrain: Flat to rolling, with a backcountry feel

Trail difficulty: Easiest

Surface quality: Ungroomed, but portions groomed by snowmobilers and skier tracked

Food and facilities: There is no water. Toilets are available along the way, as is a warming cabin and lean-to shelters. There are general stores in nearby West Wardsboro and Wardsboro. If you are coming from the Stratton Mountain Ski Area, rentals are available there, as are convenience stores. After the ski there is Norm's on Routes 30/100 in Jamaica for Italian (802–874–7004). For lodging, call Stratton Mountain Ski Area at (800) STRATTON.

Phone numbers: Manchester Ranger District of the Green Mountain National Forest, (802) 362–2307.

The loop around Grout Pond is like a pizza with your favorite toppings. Throw in a tiny slice of Vermont's state-long cross-country trail, add a handful of small rolling dips, toss in views of alpine slopes, sprinkle on some pristine pond vistas, and shake on a dab or two of warmth at a trailside cabin and shelter, and you've got a tasty adventure.

The Grout Pond Recreation Area south of Stratton Mountain has about 12 miles of interconnected trails in the Green Mountain National Forest. The network offers many opportunities for skiers and snowshoers along the easy and more difficult well-marked trails that circumnavigate the pond and lead to the shores of Somerset Reservoir. A small portion of the loop utilizes the Catamount Ski Trail, a 300-mile-long trail that runs from the Massachusetts border to Canada, roughly paralleling the Long Trail. Long Trail is maintained by the Catamount Trail Association, founded in 1985.

Not only is the Grout Pond area ski country, there are also snowmobile trails in the neighborhood. Skiers, snowshoers, and snowmobilers share the same parking area and about a 1.0-mile section of the loop. The snowmobile trails, blazed in orange, are maintained by the Vermont Association of Snow Travelers.

Winter campers, particularly those on snowshoes, can use this loop as an overnight excursion. Grout Pond is home to three lean-tos. One

lean-to is accessible via the Pond Trail and provides views of Mount Snow's ski trails.

The loop begins along Forest Road 262, also part of the Catamount Ski Trail. The superwide trail is also used by snowmobiles, which pack it. Cruise down and roll up to a junction with the East Trail and turn left. Blue diamonds show you the way. The Forest Service has excellent signs and also uses letters that correspond with its map to record distances. The trail narrows in the woods. It is here that the fun really begins—it is like riding a camel with a never-ending assortment of humps. The East Trail gives way to the Pond Trail, which circles Grout Pond. The oblong pond is to your right. Soon a lean-to will appear just off the trail on the left. Many of the views of the pond are through trees, but on occasion the vistas open up, offering a photo opportunity.

Directions at a glance

0.0 Leave the parking area, cross the road, and travel on FR 262, also known as the Catamount Ski Trail.

0.5 Turn left on the East Trail.

0.6 Turn right on the East Trail.

1.3 Turn left on the Pond Trail.

3.6 Turn right on FR 262 and travel 1.2 miles back to the parking area.

Pond Trail rounds the southeastern shore of Grout Pond and soon parts company with it. Cross over a bridge with handrails and stay with the Pond Trail as it becomes part of the Catamount again. The trail ascends along the western side of the pond, and there are wonderful respites thrown in for good measure: The Pond Trail will come out by a cabin with a toilet next to it. Head to the table and have some lunch. Continue past the cabin to another that has seen better days.

The Pond Trail leads you to FR 262 again when you bear to the right. The wide snowmobile trail returns. Follow along. A wildlife viewing area will appear on the left. Moose tracks and game birds have been spotted in the

A skier pauses on the Pond Trail around Grout Pond to reflect upon the distant ski slopes.

recreation area. The familiar East Trail will enter right. Ski the final half mile back to the parking area.

How to get there

From Waldeboro (Route 100) turn right on the Arlington–West Wardsboro Road (sign points to Stratton.) Travel through West Wardsboro and the small town of Stratton 6.5 miles to the Grout Mountain Recreation Parking Area on the right. Along the way the road becomes Kelley Stand Road (Forest Route 6).

Big Bear Loop

Grafton Ponds Nordic Ski Center, Grafton, Vermont

Type of trail:	▬ ‹ ◕
Distance:	4.7 miles
Terrain:	Rolling trails to mountain cabin
Trail difficulty:	More difficult
Surface quality:	Groomed, skate lane, double tracked
Food and facilities:	Rentals (skis and snowshoes), lessons, retail shop, snowmaking, skating, snow tubing, wax room, and cold and hot snacks are available at the touring center. There is a trail fee. For dinner try The Old Tavern Inn (800–843–1801) just down Townsend Road in Grafton. The Big Bear Cabin on this loop is an ideal lunch and warming up spot. The Grafton Village Store in the town center is handy for quick items and sandwiches or Daniels House Cafe (802–843–2255) next to the Old Tavern Inn, which also has lodging. The Grafton Village Cheese Company (next to the ski center) provides samples of its six types of cheddar (and it is possible to ski from the ski center to the cheese company).
Phone numbers:	The Grafton Ponds Nordic Ski Center, (802) 843–2400.

Time appears to stand still in the quaint community of Grafton, Vermont. Nestled in southeastern Vermont among farms and forest, the little town of 600 once subsisted on farming and logging. But the Great Depression in the 1930s put the economy on the skids. Enter the Windham Foundation, a philanthropic nonprofit historic preservation organization. It bought up much of the land and many of the buildings in the valley and has worked to revitalize the community, which is now home

to a thriving, quaint inn, cheese factory, and 20 miles of skate-friendly cross-country ski trails.

The trails at Grafton, including about 10 miles just for snowshoeing, are found in a valley between Grafton and Townsend at the base of Big Bear Mountain. The gentle ridge lines running through the hardwood and softwood forests are gateways to long, extended views down on the village with its two pert, white church steeples and neighboring hills.

The rustic Nordic center has both a fireplace and woodstove for those cold, winter days, while the Big Bear Cabin, near the midpoint on this loop, is kept warm on the weekends by its own woodstove.

Interestingly Grafton has no trails that are graded most difficult. And though the Big Bear Loop is labeled more difficult, it is only because of a couple of steep, short pitches that climb up to the cabin. Also the trails at Grafton are extremely wide, making it a winter playground for skate skiers.

Begin outside the touring center on Main Trail in front of the warm-up field. The network is well marked with signs naming the trail. Ski or snowshoe past the frozen ponds and bear left as the trail gently ascends through the birch trees. Be sure to stop at the Village Overlook for a soothing look out at the snow-covered meadows, sleepy village with woodstoves ablaze, and Spring Hill in the background. Main Trail gives way to the right to Little Bear, which has a bit more bite. Spot fox, turkey, deer, and even occasional bear tracks (not surprisingly) on the trails. Keep an eye out for them on the snow, and the hawks that circle overhead. Little Bear ascends to a winding Big Bear during the 600-foot climb to the highest point on the trail.

Directions at a glance

0.0 Leave the touring center on Main Trail and bear left about 100 yards.

0.5 Turn right on Little Bear.

1.5 Bear left on Big Bear.

4.0 Bear right on Little Bear.

4.2 Bear right on Main Trail and ski 0.5 mile back to the touring center.

Near the 2-mile mark, the small Big Bear Cabin is a welcome sight. Through the birch, spruce, and pine forest, look across to Burt Hill and try to spot Target Rock. It is said the rock was used as a marker by a man who lived in the area in the 1940s and 1950s. He flew airplanes, and the rock was like a flight tower, marking a spot close to where he could land his aircraft on a grassy runway.

The time has come for a nearly 2-mile downhill run on Big and Little Bear Trails. Leave the warmth of the cabin and continue on Big Bear for a long, easy, and winding ride. About three-quarters of a mile from the cabin, try and take a rest at the Grafton Overlook, which provides another cozy village scene. Signs point to the touring center and are easy to follow back as Big Bear weaves into Little Bear and back to Main Trail.

How to get there

From I–91 take exit 7 and follow Route 11 west some 12.3 miles. Turn left in Chester on Route 35 south. Travel on Route 35 south for some 7.4 miles. Turn right on Main Street (Route 121) in Grafton. Follow it for a few hundred yards and turn left on Townsend Road. Grafton Ponds is down the road about three-quarters of a mile.

Mount Olga Trail

Molly Stark State Park, Wilmington, Vermont

Type of trail:	⬤
Also used by:	Hikers
Distance:	2.3 miles
Terrain:	Gradual climb to uplifting fire tower
Trail difficulty:	Easiest
Surface quality:	Ungroomed
Food and facilities:	There are no facilities. Wilmington has supplies. There is a Grand Union on Route 9. Try Sonny's Cup and Saucer on Route 100 next to a general store for after the snowshoe, (802) 464–5813. For rentals, try Down in the Valley (802–464–2211), West Main Street, Wilmington. Lodging is plentiful, but for suggestions call the Mount Snow Valley Chamber of Commerce at (877) VT–SOUTH.
Phone numbers:	Winter phone number for Molly Stark State Park, (802) 886–2434.

Why climb a mountain? "Because it's there" is the famous answer. "Because of the views" is the answer for climbing the small, but fire-tower-view heavy 2,415-foot Mount Olga in southern Vermont's Molly Stark State Park. To be fair the summit on Mount Olga is actually quite cluttered. There are a few wooden maintenance shacks for the antenna perched atop the mountain. While standing on the summit, you can't see a thing.

So, what do you do?

Take off those snowshoes and start climbing the steps of the fire tower. From the enclosed tower the spectacular 360-degree panorama

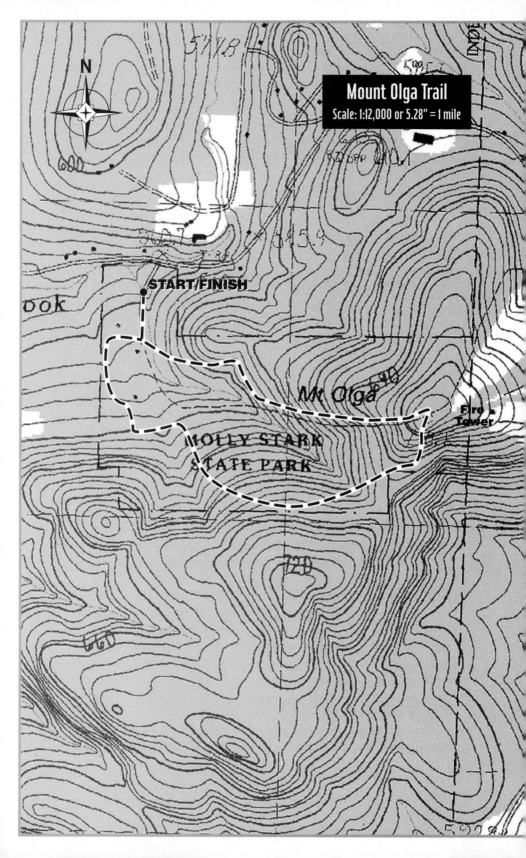

takes in portions of three states—southern Vermont, northern Massachusetts, and southwestern New Hampshire. Valley floors give way to alpine slopes. Evergreens frame each picture from the window panes in the fire tower.

The loop trail up and down Mount Olga is fairly easy, winding through the evergreens to the summit. There are a few moderate pitches along the way, but they are quickly and easily conquered.

The Mount Olga Trail is blazed in blue. Skiing it is not recommended.

The park road into the state park is the gateway to the trail. Snowshoe past the closed gate along the park road. A rushing brook parallels the snow-covered road. The brown park headquarters building is at the top of the gentle incline. The trailhead is across the building on the left side of the park road by the brook.

The trail immediately crosses a wooden bridge over the little stream and starts a gradual climb through the forest. The trail passes through stone walls twice, though they may be obscured, depending on how much snow has fallen. Soon enough you reach a junction. Here the Mount Olga Trail continues right back to the campground. Remember this junction and head up another 0.1 mile to the summit.

Climb the fire tower and drink in the views.

Descend the summit the same way and be sure to follow the Mount Olga Trail to the left back to the campground. The trail descends gradually along a stone wall. There are a couple of small stream crossings along the descent. Use the rocks to negotiate the trickling waters.

The trail heads to the campground and follows the park road back to park headquarters. As a point of reference, the first lean-to passed is named "Poplar" and the second is named "Spruce." Turn left on the park

Directions at a glance

0.0 Go around the gate at the entrance of the Molly Stark State Park and proceed along the park road.

0.2 Turn left by the sign for the Olga Mountain Trail, which is across from brown park headquarters in the park/campground, and follow it 0.8 mile to the junction.

0.9 Head straight at the signed junction to the summit. From the summit return back to junction and turn left by the sign on Olga Mountain Trail, which is a 0.9-mile path to the campground.

2.0 Turn left on the park road and follow it back to park headquarters.

2.2 Turn left on park road by park headquarters and follow it 0.2 mile back to the gate by the park entrance.

A stream rushes below the trails of Mount Olga.

road through the campground. It will sweep right and pass the familiar park headquarters building. Pass headquarters and turn left back down to the gate.

How to get there

From Wilmington travel east on Route 9 about 3.4 miles. The entrance to the Molly Stark State Park is at 3.5 miles, but the entrance is not plowed. So, at the 3.4-mile mark from Wilmington, turn left on Sparrow Lane and follow it to the plowed turnaround. Park there so as not to interfere with traffic. The entrance to the park is across Route 9.

Old Railroad Bed/West River Trail

Jamaica State Park, Jamaica, Vermont

Type of trail:	▬▬▬ ⬤
Also used by:	Winter hikers
Distance:	2.3 miles one way, 4.6 miles round-trip (optional side trip)
Terrain:	Flat adventure along the West River
Trail difficulty:	Easiest
Surface quality:	Ungroomed
Food and facilities:	There are no facilities. The Jamaica Corner Store on Route 30 has food and drink. For lodging, Ranney Brook Farm is a B&B on Route 30, West Townshend (802–874–4589). Rentals (weekends only) can be had at Townshend Outfitters on Route 30 (802–365–7308).
Phone numbers:	Winter phone number for Jamaica State Park, (802) 886–2434.

Though the railroad that once ran alongside the white-capped West River was called "36 miles of trouble," the flat and scenic section that you access through Jamaica State Park is anything but trouble. The West River Railroad chugged along between Brattleboro and Londonderry from 1879 to 1935. But the railroad had its problems. Money was tight, so it was built with cheap materials. Throw in steep terrain, sharp corners, foul weather, and cold, snowy Vermont winters and that adds up to trouble. A devastating flood in 1927 nearly wiped out the tracks, so in 1939 the tracks were torn up. The rail bed remains as the park's Old Railroad Bed/West River Trail. It is a 2-mile-wide stretch with nine nature stops filled with historical and ecological information about the area, running alongside the dark, rushing river waters, strewn with snow-capped rocks in a narrow gorge.

Pass through the dormant campground to the sleeping nature center and then the swimming area in the river. Soon the nature boxes will appear.

Ferns and carpetlike green moss grow from the huge boulders, signs of ancient glacial activity. Birches, hemlocks, spruce, ash, maple, and others fill the spectacular gorge. The interpretive signs in the boxes are an outdoor treasure trove of information. On top, each box gives a story about a particular subject. Open them up and inside is a little science lesson about the wildlife and flora and fauna that inhabit the area. There are also mileage markers that tell you the distance from the dormant nature center. Benches and picnic tables are scattered along the trails as well.

There is a sense of nature's circle of life along this trail. As winter turns to spring, the snow melts and flows into the West River, feeding it. Its churning waters then attract kayakers. Even before the Ball Mountain Dam was built upriver, whitewater enthusiasts came here to test their skills. Now they come in April and September to challenge the roiling waters.

The water is your constant companion during this flat adventure. The easiness of the trail, rest stops, and nature signs make this trip ideal for families with children. They will also enjoy the mini-waterfalls along the way.

If you are here in late winter as spring approaches, you'll hear the waters' thunderous tone. For a most dramatic vantage point, go where the trail and river bend hard to the left, a point called the "Ox bow," between stations five and six. At station six learn about this U-shaped bend created by erosion.

It should be noted that the West River Trail accesses the Hamilton Falls Trail, which leads to one of the most beautiful waterfalls in the state. Hamilton Falls drops 125 feet and becomes a frozen masterpiece in winter. The trail to the falls is a long, moderate 1.2-mile climb along an old road high atop Cobb Brook. It is for better snowshoers. The trail to the falls leaves right at 1.9 miles. The falls have claimed at least ten lives in recent years, a nearby sign notes.

Station nine marks the end of this West River Trail adventure. The bench is a fine place to watch Cobb Brook flow into the West River by the old stone bridge abutments. Rest up and return along the same route.

Directions at a glance

0.0 Leave the plowed out parking area of Jamaica State Park by going around the gate and through the campground, which parallels the West River.

0.3 Leave the day camping area by a sign that points to a number of trails: Railroad Bed Trail, Bald Mountain Dam, Overlook Trail, Hamilton Falls. Go straight.

2.2 Turn right at Hamilton Falls Trail for optional out-and-back moderate snowshoe to falls.

2.3 Reach the end of the trail by station 9 and the bench. Return the same way.

How to get there

From Jamaica turn on Depot Street and follow it 0.5 mile past the school, over the bridge, and to the small plowed-out parking area on the left.

new hampshire

B&M Trail

Bretton Woods, New Hampshire

Type of trail:	══ ＜ ⬤
Distance:	7.5 miles; a shorter 5.0-mile loop option
Terrain:	Flat to rolling adventure in Presidential neighborhood
Trail difficulty:	Easiest to more difficult
Surface quality:	Groomed, single tracked, double tracked
Food and facilities:	Cross-country and snowshoe rentals, instruction, a snack bar called the Nordic Cafe, wax room, and rest rooms are available at the Bretton Woods Cross-Country Ski Center inside the Mount Washington Hotel; trail passes are also sold in the center. No food or water is available during the tour. There is a heated yurt about midway. Nearby Fabyan's Station (603–278–2222), a renovated train station, serves lunch and dinner and inside the Hotel, itself a marvelous place to spend the night, is Stickney's Restaurant.
Phone numbers:	Number for Bretton Woods, (603) 278–3320; direct line to the cross-country center, (603) 278–3322.

With an impressive backdrop of the rugged snow-capped Presidential Range and the beauty of the red-roofed Mount Washington Hotel, the Bretton Woods Cross-Country Ski Center serves up more than 60 miles of trails for skiers and snowshoers.

Some 80 percent of visitors stick to the Ammonoosuc Trail System with its network of wide, flat beginner trails and friendly intermediate routes. This loop utilizes that system. The Deception System has more varied and challenging terrain, including a trail that traverses Mount Deception. The Stickney System is the lift-served network found by the slopes of the downhill ski area, which includes the curves of Mountain Road. The Perimeter Trail, double tracked with a skate lane in the middle, circumnavigates a golf course, offering a flat, open route with majestic views of the mountains and hotel. (The hotel, complete with a railed veranda sweeping around its white face, opened in 1902 and is now a National Historic Landmark.)

The Ammonoosuc flows from Mount Washington, the Northeast's highest peak at 6,288 feet, and parallels the B&M Trail for a spell. The B&M trail follows an abandoned railroad bed—the line once used to access the Cog Railroad—which goes to the top of Mount Washington. The B&M is primarily a straight shot through the woods, with a few rollers near the end.

B & M Trail

Scale: 1:25,000 or 2.53" = 1 mile

The historic Mount Washington Hotel is set in front of a Presidential backdrop on the Bretton Woods Cross-Country network.

The B&M enters the woods. It is narrow and tunnel-like, lined with firs. Look down on the pools of water during the gentle ascent. Though there is a skate lane, skate skiers might prefer the wider Bridle Path that parallels the B&M and later rejoins it. The Bridle Path dates back to the 1800s when it was used as a horse path. A short side trip well worth taking is the 50-foot jaunt off the B&M to Upper Falls. Here a bridge and gorge team up for a glorious view of the summit of Mount Monroe.

About midway through the loop, you'll find a heated yurt with Mount Washington views. The Porcupine Lane is more playful and has a few interesting curves. About 0.5 mile into Porcupine Lane, the route begins its descent (some 500 feet has been gained in elevation during this tour). Round a bend on Porcupine and come to a junction with Sebosis, a trail labeled more difficult, no doubt due to its winding, snakelike downhill. Sebosis is a blast as it winds its way back down to the flats. Firs and birches line the trail. Several wide and easy bridge crossings over brooks are part of the descent. You leave the sheltered woods behind where Sebosis rejoins the flats of the Perimeter Trail where the Presidentials stand guard over the rear of the hotel. You can take a shorter, equally scenic tour of about 5.0 miles by combining a

Directions at a glance

0.0 Leave the cross-country ski center via the Perimeter Trail. There is one section where skiers should take off skis before crossing a hotel road.

0.5 Follow the Perimeter Trail. It will merge with a connector trail that points the way to the B&M Trail.

1.0 Bear left on the B&M Trail and follow it for some 3.0 miles.

4.0 Turn right on Porcupine Lane.

4.7 Turn right on Sebosis.

6.7 Stay straight on the Perimeter Trail leading back to the cross-country center.

Alternative loop

0.0 Leave the cross-country ski center via the Perimeter Trail.

0.5 Turn left on Perimeter and cross Stone Pillar Bridge.

0.8 Turn left on Bridle Path, which merges (after 1.3 miles) with B&M Trail.

2.3 Turn left to Upper Falls Bridge. Return to B&M Trail.

2.5 Turn right on B&M Trail.

4.0 Turn right on Perimeter, which leads to the hotel.

loop of the Bridle Path and B&M. This loop shaves about 2.5 miles from the aforementioned trip.

How to get there

From I–93 north take exit 35 (Route 3 north) to Route 302 east. The cross-country ski center is based near the Mount Washington Hotel.

Canal Trail

The Balsams, Dixville Notch, New Hampshire

Type of trail:	▬▬ ◄
Distance:	7.4 miles; option exists for additional 2.0-mile loop
Terrain:	Gradual incline with rewarding downhill along one of the state's premier hotel properties
Trail difficulty:	Easiest
Surface quality:	Groomed, rolled, single tracked, double tracked
Food and facilities:	A trail fee is required for access to The Balsams' cross-country trails (not for registered hotel guests). Cross-country skis and snowshoes are available for rent inside the hotel; instruction and a wax room are also available. Snowshoeing is not allowed on the cross-country trails, but is allowed on about 15 miles of snowshoe-only trails. A warming hut is an ideal lunch spot. Toilet facilities are located outside the warming hut. Food and water are not available during the ski, so bring your own. For post-ski sustenance there is the elegant Balsams. Or try burgers at Errol Restaurant and Pub some 9 miles away (603–482–3852).
Phone numbers:	Three telephone numbers for The Balsams: toll-free in the continental U.S. and Canada, (800) 255–0600; toll-free in New Hampshire, (800) 255–0800; also a general business number, (603) 255–3400.

The 50 miles of numbered cross-country trails at The Balsams Grand Resort Hotel in northern New Hampshire are set amidst the majesty of the dramatic cliffs of Dixville Notch and the grandeur of the resort itself. The northeast quadrant of the network is home to miles of groomed beginner trails, centering on the remote Mud Pond as a destination. Though this tour gains 500 feet in elevation, the gentle climb along the tree-guarded trails is but a memory after a rest stop in a toasty warming hut along the pond's frozen shores.

History and nature hold a friendly competition for the skier's attention because the tour is filled with both. The well-protected Golf Course Road Trail (no. 0) makes a slow ascent through sugar maples, passing the Two Town Pond. The pond used to be part of the irrigation system for local farms. Beavers prefer it now. You also have distant views of Canada's Mount Hereford and Vermont's Mount Monadnock. The Moose Pond Trail, which follows Moose Brook, traverses the northern base of Mount Abenaki, where rare peregrine falcons soar in March.

Directions at a glance

0.0   Begin at the Golf Course Road trailhead and ski the well-signed Golf Course Road Trail (no. 0).

1.5   Turn right on Moose Pond Trail (no. 12)—there is a sign—and ski it for 1.0 mile.

2.5   Turn right at the sign for the Tunnel Trail (no. 10) and ski about .25 mile to the top of the hill.

2.75   At the top of the hill, make a sharp left on the Valley Trail (no. 14) and ski down about 30 yards to the Canal Trail (no. 8).

2.75   Turn right on the Canal Trail (no. 8) and follow it 1.2 miles to Mud Pond.

3.9   At Mud Pond turn left on the Mud Pond Loop Trail (no. 24) and ski about 60 yards to the warming hut. As an option skiers might want to ski the entire Mud Pond Loop Trail (no. 24) clockwise. The 2.0-mile loop offers fine sporadic views of the pond.

3.9   From the Mud Pond Loop Trail, turn left on Moose Pond Trail (no. 12) and ski it about 2.0 miles, staying straight at the various intersections along the way.

5.9   Turn left on the Golf Course Road Trail (no. 0) and ski it approximately 1.5 miles back to the trailhead where the loop began.

The Tunnel and Valley Trails, the short intermediate bursts on the loop, are the gateways to a most pleasant ski—the Canal Trail. Perhaps it should be called "Christmas Tree Lane" because it winds narrowly through a forest of balsam firs. The trail, which is groomed for both classic and skate skiers, runs parallel to a hand-cut canal that once brought water from Mud Pond to the hotel. The Canal Trail is a rare treat, giving the illusion of traversing a ridge. Relax a bit at the heated warming hut on the southwest corner of Mud Pond. Plump Canada jays may coax you out of a snack. The option exists here for a 2-mile easy ski around the pond. Keep eyes alert for moose tracks if you go. The views on the northern edge of the pond are worth the trip.

The elevation at Mud Pond is 2,322 feet, a gain of nearly 500 feet in altitude from the hotel, set at 1,846 feet. Now comes time for the reward. Revisit the Moose Pond Trail. The ski begins as a downhill. But don't put all of that energy away. There are a few little pulls to negotiate. After the downhill enjoy a cruise along the wide path as Moose Pond Trail yields

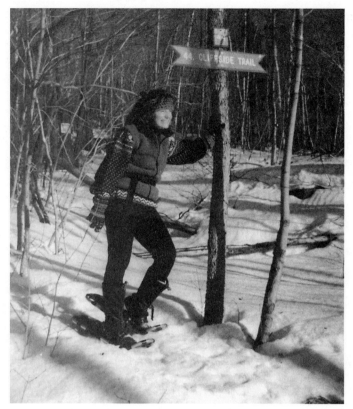

A snowshoer takes in the views on the Cliffside Trail, one of many snowshoe-only trails at The Balsams resort.

back to the Golf Course Road Trail. Gaze into the distance of Dixville Notch. It is along this trail that skiers can see why a mountain pass is called a "notch" in New Hampshire. The V-shaped cut is obvious, as are the steep sides of the narrow notch.

How to get there

From Boston head north on I–93 past Franconia Notch to exit 35, then Route 3 to Colebrook, and east on Route 26 to Dixville Notch (210 miles). Park in The Balsams' lot. Trail passes are sold inside the hotel at the cross-country center. It is then a five-minute walk to the well-signed trailhead.

Hayes Copp Ski Trail/Leavitt's Link

Gorham, New Hampshire

Type of trail:	▬▬▬ ⬭
Also used by:	Hikers
Distance:	5.0 miles
Terrain:	Flat to rolling ride on the edge of wilderness
Trail difficulty:	Easiest, more difficult
Surface quality:	Ungroomed, skier tracked
Food and facilities:	Public telephones and toilets are available near the trailhead. Winter camping is open at Barnes Field, also near the trailhead. Vehicles must display the White Mountain National Forest user fee sticker required to park. After the ski, try the Fortune Cookie (603–466–2828) on Main Street in Gorham next to the Gorham Motor Inn (603–466–3381). Gorham also has a few shops for ski and snowshoe rentals like Moriah Sports, 101 Main Street (603–466–5050).
Phone numbers:	White Mountain National Forest's Androscoggin Ranger Station for skiing conditions, (603) 466–2713; the station, just north of the trailhead on Route 16, has a wealth of information and interpretive displays. New Hampshire State Police, (800) 525–5555.

Hayes and Dolly Copp were a couple of tourism pioneers, though at the time they probably didn't know it. In 1827 Hayes traveled up through Pinkham Notch, spotted a place along the flats of the Peabody River that he thought might make a good farm, and cleared the land. Fours years later, he had a wife named Dolly, a one-room cabin, and some crops. The next thing you know they have four children and a farm and have started to greet visitors traveling to Mount Washington. Now a ski trail is named after Hayes, and a campground after Dolly.

Much of the Hayes Copp Cross-Country Ski Trail is on logging roads, a beginner's delight. Though there is an 8.0-mile network that borders the Great Gulf Wilderness, the 5.0-mile loop is a fine outing for many a skier and snowshoer. The east side of the loop, including Leavitt's Link, is largely flat and inviting. Then it heads away from the hibernating Dolly Copp Campground and into the woods to climb oh-so-gently on the Great Gulf Link with an occasional herringbone along the Peabody River. This section is quiet and peaceful, unless a large truck happens to be huffing by on Route 16, and the river's frozen waters are a pleasure to the eye. But we are getting ahead of ourselves.

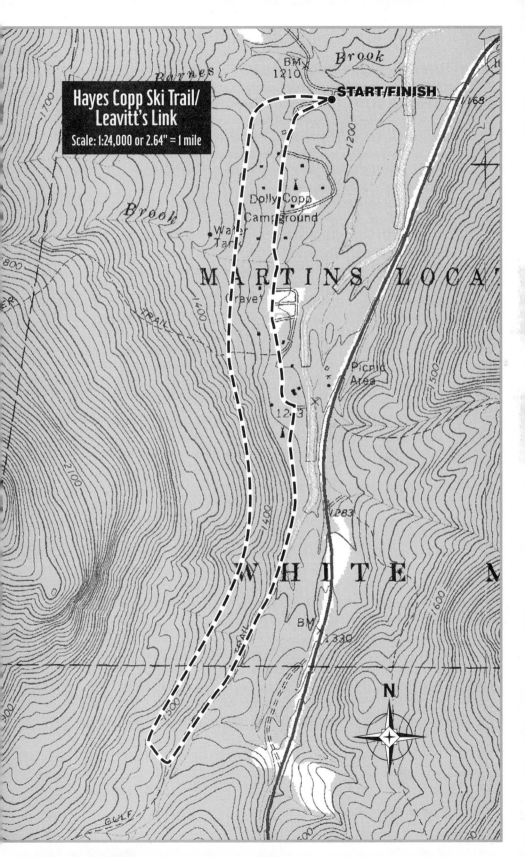

Hayes Copp Ski Trail/
Leavitt's Link
Scale: 1:24,000 or 2.64" = 1 mile

START/FINISH

Dolly Copp
Campground

Water
Tank

Brook

Barnes

Brook

MARTINS LOCAT

Gravel

Picnic
Area

TRAIL

1283

WHITE N

BM
1.330

N

GULF

The tour begins from the well-marked Dolly Copp Campground. Sign in before the tour! Then ski—or snowshoe—through the sleeping campground with snow-covered picnic tables, taps, garbage bins, and fields. Initally, the trail along the road is flat and very wide. It is marked with plastic blue squares. The outline of the Carter Range into Pinkham Notch is quite obvious to your left. Look for the Imp Profile, a cliff on a west spur of North Carter. At about the 0.5-mile mark you cross the Culhane Brook via a bridge. On the right sharp eyes can spot the cap of 4,890-foot Mount Madison. Ski right by the Daniel Webster Scout Trail, which leads to that very mountain.

There is an option shortly after the Webster Trail. Though it is not obvious, a ski trail bears to the right. Don't fret if you miss it. Stay on the campground road until it ends at the Great Gulf Link. Now, the trail enters the woods and narrows, riding

Directions at a glance

0.0 Leave trailhead, following signs for Hayes Copp Ski Trail.

0.7 Turn right on Great Gulf Link Trail.

1.3 Great Gulf Trail enters, bear right.

2.4 Turn right on Leavitt's Link Trail.

3.8 Hayes Copp Ski Trail reenters, stay straight and follow trail back to parking lot.

along the banks of the Peabody. The ski tracks may be finished for a while as hikers and snowshoers share this corridor. Perhaps a snowshoe hare will dart by. In the woods occasional signs with Nordic skiers are posted on trees. The trail follows the river and climbs a tad more steeply as it continues along the Great Gulf Trail, which it diverges from at Leavitt's Link. Beginners might consider heading back along the same way because Leavitt's Link rolls more and has some climbs. A sign at this junction outlines all the trails and distances. Turn right and climb up to a clearing on Leavitt's Link. Here are panoramic views of the Carter Range and glimpes of the Presidentials. This is a fine spot for a snack. Look for a couple of stumps that are usually there by a firepit. Get refueled because the trail will roll. There will be more than twenty bridge crossings after this point. Just after a large, fresh snowfall, you'll hardly notice the small bridges. But if conditions are icy, steel nerves help. Leavitt's Link is hilly and seems to go along the outline of the Carter Range. The trail is very easy to follow and leads back to the parking lot. Ski or snowshoe it for about 1.5 miles before the Hayes Copp Trail returns from the left. One-half mile later, after crossing a bridge over the Culhane Brook, look closely to the right for a water tank in the trees. This is a zippy little option. By taking a right just before the water tank, you can ski downhill back to the campground road. Or ignore the option, go straight, and enjoy the ride back down to the parking lot.

How to get there

From Gorham travel south on Route 16 approximately 5 miles to the Pinkham "B" Road and turn left. Travel a few hundred yards and turn left to the plowed parking area at the Dolly Copp Campground.

From Glen travel north on Route 16 about 19 miles and turn left on the Pinkham "B" Road.

Mount Willard Trail
Crawford Notch, New Hampshire

Type of trail:	
Also used by:	Hikers
Distance:	1.6 miles one way; 3.2 miles round-trip
Terrain:	Gradual climb to stellar overlook
Trail difficulty:	Easiest
Surface quality:	Ungroomed
Food and facilities:	Snowshoe rentals, rest rooms, and water are available at the Appalachian Mountain Club's Crawford Notch Hostel, Route 302, Crawford Notch. Bring food and water on the trail. After the snowshoe tour try Fabyan's (603–278–2222) near Bretton Woods or the Red Parka Pub (603–383–4344) in Glen.
Phone numbers:	Crawford Notch Hostel (603–278–5170) or the Appalachian Mountain Club's Pinkham Notch Visitor Center (603–466–2721) for trail conditions; New Hampshire State Police, (800) 525–5555.

On a winter's day the views through Crawford Notch from the ledges of Mount Willard are unsurpassed. The eagle's eye panorama takes up the whole sky. In the distance Mount Chocorua's cone rises. A snake appears to be slithering along the valley floor, but that is no reptile. It's Route 302. The scars of a slide that killed the Willey family in 1826 are evident on the flanks of Mount Willey. In the east Mount Jackson stands firm; a glimpse of the Presidential Range and Mount Washington are your rewards for looking beyond Mount Jackson.

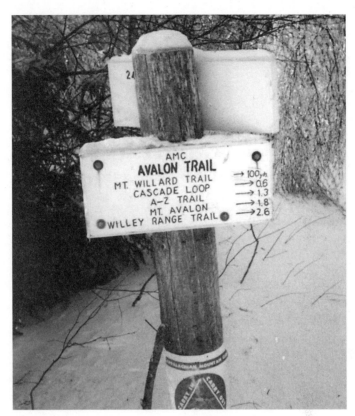

A sign points the way to the beginning of the Mount Willard Trail.

During summer and fall the Mount Willard Trail—maintained by the Appalachian Mountain Club—is a popular way up the 2,850-foot mountain. Your easy effort will yield rich and inspirational bounties. In winter the prize is equal. For those looking for a moonlight snowshoe trip, this is the one.

The trail by snowshoe is on the harder side of easy. The trailhead is across the road from Saco Lake, the source of the Saco River, which flows to the Atlantic. It is behind the brightly painted Crawford Depot, an information center during the nonsnow months. The old train station once served passengers going through the notch. In summer the Conway Scenic Railroad ends its run through the notch here. Past the tracks the trail begins with a flat walk in the woods.

The gradual ascent starts a short time later as the trail enters Crawford Notch State Park and follows a wide, carriage road, which at one time transported guests from the Crawford House, lost to a 1977 fire. At about the 0.5-mile mark, a sign points to the freezing waters of Centennial Pool off to the right. As the trail continues through the evergreens and birches, the wooded tops of two 4,000 footers—Mounts Tom and Field—can be spotted through the trees on the right. Near the top, a trail to Hitchcock Flume enters from the left. From there it is just a few more yards to the vantage point. The views, on a clear day, burst out after you've snowshoed a trail sheltered by trees.

From the ledges look out through Crawford Notch, said to be discovered by a Lancaster hunter, Timothy Nash, during a 1771 moose hunt. The blemishes on Mount Willey are evident and are reminders of the tragic 1826 landslide. The Willeys, a family of seven with five children, lived by the base of Mount Willey. A drought that summer and the heavy rains that followed are thought to have triggered the rock slide. The family fled the house. The bodies of Samuel Willey, his wife, two children, and two boarders were found. Those of the three other children were not. Ironically the house withstood the storm. The Willey House site, a few miles from the Mount Willard trailhead, tells the history of the event.

Directions at a glance

0.0 Begin on the well-signed trail that leaves from behind the Crawford Notch Depot, some 125 yards from the Crawford Notch Hostel. The Mount Willard Trail follows the Avalon Trail for about 100 yards.

0.1 The trail bears left at a sign that reads MT. WILLARD. Some 100 yards later the trail bears right by a sign for Crawford Notch State Park. Follow the trail another 1.5 miles to the ledges.

1.6 Return along the same trail.

When out on the ledges, just be sure not to go too close to the edge. To return follow the same trail as it descends easily back to the trailhead.

How to get there

From I–93 take exit 35, Route 3, north to Twin Mountain; then Route 302 east to Crawford Notch. From Glen take Route 302 west to Crawford Notch. Park by the Crawford Depot.

Nineteen-Mile Brook Trail

Pinkham Notch, New Hampshire

Type of trail:	(symbol)
Also used by:	Hikers
Distance:	3.8 miles one way; 7.6 miles round-trip
Terrain:	Initally flat, then a gradual climb with a few steep pitches
Trail difficulty:	More difficult
Surface quality:	Ungroomed, but packed
Food and facilities:	Use the Appalachian Mountain Club's Carter Notch Hut, near the frozen shores of Carter Pond, to warm up, rest, and eat the food you have carried with you. Water is available, but carry extra. Hot water is also available, but carry tea, coffee, or hot chocolate. Overnight accommodations can be had, making this a welcome overnight experience (bring your own sleeping bag). The hut sleeps forty and has a caretaker in winter. Reservations are suggested. White Mountain National Forest (WMNF) pass needed at trailhead.
Phone numbers:	Appalachian Mountain Club's Pinkham Notch Visitor Center (603–466–2721) for reservations for the hut; information from the U.S. Forest Service's Androscoggin Ranger Station, (603) 466–2713; New Hampshire State Police, (800) 525–5555.

To be in Carter Notch in winter is to experience a feeling of being remote and wild. The impressive pass between the 4,422-foot Wildcat Mountain and the 4,832-foot Carter Dome is the result of a glacial tug-of-war, with huge ice sheets carving out the gap while shaking massive boulders from the tops of the surrounding peaks. In the notch are two frozen ponds—Upper and Lower Carter Ponds—surrounded and dwarfed by the foreboding landscape.

The Appalachian Mountain Club's Carter Notch Hut is at 3,290 feet above sea level and is sandwiched between the two ponds. When the frigid winds blow, the hut is a welcome sanctuary. The AMC first built a small log cabin in the notch in 1904. It was replaced by a stone hut in 1914. It is said the present hut is haunted by the ghost of a former care-taker, "Red Mac" MacGregor.

Because of the hut this snowshoe trip (skiers can attempt this trail, but it is steep in places and the sporadic drainages may interrupt rhythm) is a natural for an overnight. Adjacent to the hut are bunkhouses. The hut is warmed by a wood stove. Therefore if you are using backpacks, bring sleeping bags rated to at least minus 20 degrees.

START/FINISH

Garnet Pool

E N S   G R A N T

River

Glen House

BM
563

AQUEDUCT   X 1913   PATH

Brook

Little Wildcat Mtn

BM
2322

CARTER

N

Brook

B

DOME

T

Carter Notch   **Cabin**
3388

Nineteen-Mile Brook Trail
Scale: 1:24,000 or 2.64" = 1 mile

The Nineteen-Mile Brook Trail, which is well marked and leaves from the trailhead on Route 16, is also popular with winter hikers. Though the trail is ungroomed, it is the combination of hikers and snowshoers that packs it down. Midweek travelers will likely relish the solitude. Weekenders will likely have more company.

Not only is the trail popular, but the brook itself is also worth experiencing. It is a beautiful site as it rises easily through the forest. The brook's chilled waters form pools in certain spots, trapped by the boulders that stand in its path.

As the trail continues it narrows and comes very close to the water's edge. Portions of the path near the brook can become icy during winter, so caution is suggested. A small hut and stone dam can be seen at about the 1.2-mile mark as the trail rises up above the waters. You cross several drainages before reaching the midway point. The Carter Dome Trail will diverge from the left at 1.9 miles, marking midway to Carter Notch.

Following the junction with the Carter Dome Trail, the trail begins to climb, steeply at times. You'll have to negotiate two narrow footbridges over the course of about 0.3 mile.

Through the trees spot the ridges of Wildcat Mountain. Steep pitches alternate with a few flat spots as the trail reaches its highest point at the 3.6-mile mark. Here Wildcat Ridge Trail enters.

Nineteen-Mile Brook Trail takes a sharp left and drops steeply through the firs. It is here that nature raises its curtain on a dramatic scene. From the woods the stage is set for a view of the western shores of Upper Carter Pond. Wildcat Mountain rises up like a giant wall. The trail hugs the bank and then reenters the woods where you'll pass the Carter-Moriah Trail. A few steps take you out to the northwest edge of Lower Carter Pond. Look up in the natural amphitheater and see the crags of Carter Dome. Just to the right of the dome is Pulpit Rock, still defying gravity.

Directions at a glance

0.0 Leave the trailhead via the Nineteen-Mile Brook Trail.

1.2 Spot a dam by the brook.

1.9 Carter Dome Trail enters from the left. Continue straight. Cross two narrow footbridges over the next 0.3 mile.

3.6 Turn left on the Nineteen-Mile Brook Trail, which drops steeply.

3.8 Carter-Moriah Trail enters from the left. Continue on the Nineteen-Mile Brook Trail.

3.9 Reach the hut. Stay the night or return via the same trail.

The Carter Notch Hut, though allegedly haunted by the friendly spirit of a former caretaker, is a welcome stop on the Nineteen-Mile Brook Trail.

Snowshoers reach the hut after the second pond. Inside they can warm and refuel themselves before hunkering down for the night or returning along the same trail, which is right outside the hut's door.

How to get there

From Glen travel 16 miles north on Route 16. The trailhead is on the right. From Gorham travel about 7 miles south on Route 16. The trailhead is on the left.

Great Angel Loop/Great Glen Trails

Pinkham Notch, New Hampshire

Type of trail:	➖ ❮ ⬭
Distance:	4.2 miles
Terrain:	Flat to rolling ski in the shadow of Mount Washington
Trail difficulty:	More difficult
Surface quality:	Groomed, skate, double tracked
Food and facilities:	Rentals (ski and snowshoe), lessons, a wax room, restaurant, retail shop, and tubing are all found at Great Glen (with water available at the yurts). Rest rooms are outside of the yurts. In addition Great Glen offers a snowcoach sightseeing service to the 4-mile mark on the Mount Washington Auto Road for a round-trip ride or free-heel ski down. There is a fee to use the ski center trails. After skiing it's possible to dine at the timber base lodge or try the Red Parka Pub (603–383–4344) in Glen.
Phone numbers:	Great Glen Trails, (603) 466–2333.

They say location is everything. Great Glen Trails is located at the base of one of the most picturesque spots in New Hampshire—Mount Washington. The highest peak in the northeastern United States serves as a backdrop along with a few of its more dramatic sidekicks, Mounts Jefferson, Adams, and Madison. Throw in wide, open meadows with winding, well-groomed runs through the beech, birch, and pines; views of the jagged Moriah-Carter Range to the east; vistas of the alpine slopes of Wildcat Mountain; and a couple of woodstove-heated yurts, and you've got the makings for winter fun.

Great Glen Trails opened on December 26, 1994. There are about 12 miles of skate and tracked trails. Snowshoes are allowed on all of the trails plus the 12 miles of backcountry trails that border the Great Gulf Wilderness on a side of Mount Washington. Only a small portion of the groomed network is classified as most difficult. The system is well signed. Trail names are given in both English and French. The trail names are a bit humorous and clever, too. There's the Great Grumpy Grade, which got its name because the trail took a bit longer to construct than anticipated, annoying the construction crew, which became a tad grumpy during work. Dragon Corridor got its name because with its twists, turns, and bumps, it resembles a dragon's tail.

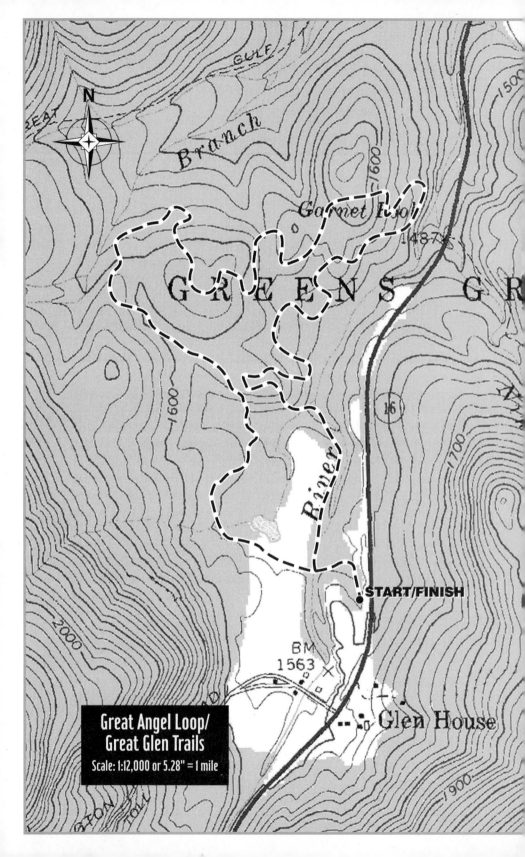

N

GULF

GREAT

Branch

Garnet Hjol

1600

1487

GREENS   GR

1600

1500

16

1700

River

2000

START/FINISH

BM
1563

1900

Glen House

GTON TOLL

**Great Angel Loop/
Great Glen Trails**
Scale: 1:12,000 or 5.28" = 1 mile

With the Presidentials as a backdrop, the groomed trails of Great Glen Trails are pathways to adventure.

Great Angel Loop is flat to rolling circuit. The loop is a collection of many easy and more difficult trails. The difficulty is not in the ascents—they are gradual—but in the exhilarating and winding downhills.

From the lodge the easy Geepers Trail leads to Great Meadows Sluice, which crosses over the flowing Peabody River and is the gateway to the ski system. Sluice links to Great Grumpy Grade, which offers stunning vistas of the snow-topped and craggy northern Presidentials from the flats of an alpine meadow. Grumpy enters the woods and hands off to Libby Trace by a huge granite slab called Coffee Pot Rock. Dawdle a bit at the rock and look at the old coffee pots on it. They were found when the trail system was built. By the way, Libby Trace is named after Elihu Libby. He bought the Auto Road in 1906, and his descendants still own the road and Great Glen. Libby is a gradual rollick.

The snakelike Dragon Corridor is next. Slay the trail by riding the winding path where bear, moose, and bobcat have been spotted. Dragon Corridor weaves into Peacemaker and Thumper. Both these trails drop and climb dramatically. Thumper has a picnic table for those who want to rest a bit after the roller coaster ride.

Wishbone Slip is like a switchback, the U-shaped turn provides excitement right into Hairball Passage. Hairball passes over a swampy area and gets its name from the population of snowshoe hares that frequents the area.

A short jaunt, Fuzzbottom Brake, leads to the flat and open Clementine Wash, which parallels the Peabody River, a drainage flowing out of Pinkham Notch and into the Androscoggin River. Clementine flows back to Sluice, which is the path back to the lodge.

How to get there

From North Conway, New Hampshire, travel west on Routes 16/302 to Glen. Turn right at traffic light on Route 16 north and travel approximately 12 miles to Great Glen on the left. From Gorham, New Hampshire, travel south on Route 16 to Great Glen approximately 8 miles on the right.

Directions at a glance

0.0 Leave the lodge on Geepers Trail.

0.2 Turn left at Glen Meadows Sluice.

0.4 Continue on Great Grumpy Grade.

0.7 Turn right on Libby Trace.

1.4 Bear right on Dragon Corridor.

1.9 Bear left on Peacemaker.

2.1 Bear right on Thumper.

2.9 Continue straight on Wishbone Slip.

3.2 Turn left on Hairball Passage.

3.3 Turn left on Fuzzbottom Brake.

3.4 Turn right on Clementine Wash.

3.8 Turn left on Glen Meadows Sluice.

4.0 Turn right on Geepers and travel 0.2 mile to lodge.

Fire Tower Trail

Phillips Brook Backcountry Recreation Area, Stark, New Hampshire

Type of trail:	
Also used by:	Hikers, backcountry skiers, dogsledders
Distance:	5.6 miles round-trip
Terrain:	Flat to hilly backwoods trek to fire tower
Trail difficulty:	More difficult
Surface quality:	Groomed after snowstorms
Food and facilities:	There are portable toilets at the field office for day users. No water is available on the trail. There are toilets at the 11 yurts in the area. Stop in Gorham or Berlin at the many grocery stores for food. A fire tower makes an ideal spot for a backpack lunch. After the outing consider the lunch and dinner buffets at the Fortune Cookie (603–466–2828) on Main Street in Gorham. Ovenight opportunities abound at the yurts and lodge.
Phone numbers:	Phillips Brook Backcountry Recreation Area, (800) 872–4578.

Near the roof of New Hampshire is a place where the moose, deer, and fisher mingle with the logger, snowshoer, backcountry skier, and sled dog driver. It is called the Phillips Brook Backcountry Recreation Area and is a unique partnership on 24,000 acres in the remote northern section of the state called the Great North Woods.

In 1997 a North Conway, New Hampshire, company called Mountain Recreation entered into an agreement with International Paper for rights to operate the recreation area on land owned by the paper company. While loggers continue their harvest, backcountry enthusiasts can play on the land that abuts the state's 45,000-acre Nash Stream State Forest.

Skiers and snowshoers are given free access to the 135 miles of trails, which are primarily logging roads and multiuse trails. Mountain Recreation makes its money by running a lodge and net-

Makeshift signs point the way at the Phillips Brook Backcountry Recreation Area.

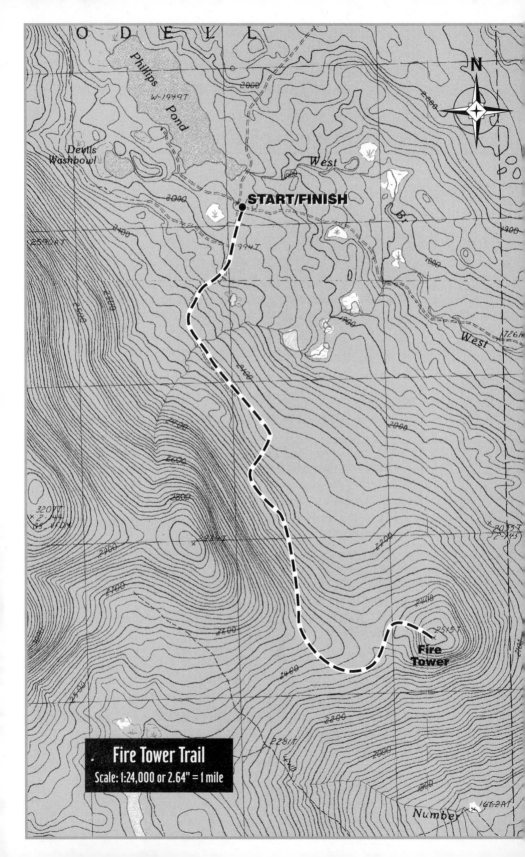

O D E L L

Phillips
Pond
w-1949T

Devils
Washbowl

West

START/FINISH

N

Fire
Tower

Fire Tower Trail
Scale: 1:24,000 or 2.64" = 1 mile

Number

work of yurts that skiers, hikers, and showshoers can use. During the nonsnow months, mountain bikers and hikers use the miles of trails and yurts.

Make no mistake, this is a remote, backcountry experience. Even getting to the trailheads can be an adventure for some along a snow-covered dirt road. Logging gates are sometimes locked, and the combinations must be obtained from the Phillips Brook field office before recreationists can proceed.

The trails are well defined through grooming and use; however, do not use the multicolored plastic ribbons tied to the trees as trail markers. These flags are used by the paper company to indicate harvest areas and proposed routes.

Directions at a glance

0.0 Leave the trailhead on the Trio Ponds Trail.

2.1 Turn right on the Trio Ponds Trail at the junction with the Gorge Trail.

2.4 Turn left on the Fire Tower Trail and travel 0.4 mile to the fire tower.

2.8 Return via the same route.

While out on the trails, keep an eye out for wildlife. Even if you do not spot some creatures, it is commonplace to spot the deep tracks of a moose or their round droppings.

The outing begins with a gradual ascent through the hardwood forest on the northeast side of Whitcomb Mountain. As elevation increases, so does the damage done by the ice storm of January 1998. The storm's wrath was vengeful, splintering trees like toothpicks and toppling the crowns of many a hardwood. Birch trees seem to bow out of respect.

A traverse, with views across to Owl Head and Kelsey Mountains, takes skiers and snowshoers just below the saddle that connects the fire tower to the mountain. A few switchbacks later, you leave the Trio Ponds Trail for the winding Fire Tower Trail. The Trio Ponds Trail is a fine choice for a side trip as it is 1.3 miles to Trio Ponds Yurt and an overnight backcountry experience.

The fire tower was built in the early 1950s by International Paper as a way to look out over the Phillips Brook Valley and keep an eye on company holdings. The wintry panaorama extends into the Mahoosucs of Maine and the Moriahs and regal Presidentials of New Hampshire to the south. Dummer and Trio Ponds glimmer in the distance.

The real fun for skiers begins on the return trip to the trailhead. The Fire Tower Trail twists and winds down moderately to the junction with the Trio Ponds Trail. The switchbacks are now a series of exhilarating S-turns. As the trip ends, the final third of a mile back to the trailhead is a wide cruise back to the road.

How to get there

From Berlin travel north approximately 18 miles to Paris Road in West Milan. Turn right on Paris Road and drive 3.5 miles to the Paris Road office of Timberland Trails. Four-wheel-drive vehicles are recommended during winter travel. At the field office get the handout that provides the combinations to the gates along the road. Follow the signs to the Phillips Brook Lodge. The trailhead for the Trio Ponds Trail is approximately 10 miles in on the left.

Boulder Loop Trail
Albany, New Hampshire

Type of trail:	
Also used by:	Hikers
Distance:	3.0 miles
Terrain:	Hilly circuit laced with much to explore
Trail difficulty:	Easiest
Surface quality:	Ungroomed
Food and facilities:	Toilets are available at the winter parking area. No water is available during the loop. You'll need a White Mountain National Forest Recreation Pass to park in the winter parking area. You can rent snowshoes at the Kancamagus Snowshoe Center (Baldy's) on Route 112, Conway, (603) 447–5287. You can do your grocery shopping in Conway. After the loop, try Cafe Noche, Main Street, Conway (603–447–5050). The Albert B. Lester Memorial Hostel, Washington Street, Conway (603–447–1001), is clean and inexpensive.
Phone numbers:	White Mountain National Forest's Saco Ranger District, (603) 447–5448.

The Boulder Loop Trail is a shining example of how a popular summer and fall hike can turn into an excellent winter snowshoe excursion. The 3.0-mile trail rewards the snowshoer with spectacular vistas above the Passaconaway Valley for a relatively modest amount of effort. Not only that, the mammoth glaciers that moved through the area some 50,000 years ago left large, granite boulders behind that are transformed into towering jewels of ice in winter. One of the massive slabs measures 30 feet high and 100 feet long. There is even one spot on the loop where it is possible to snowshoe under a boulder for a cavelike experience.

The yellow-blazed trail reaches its highest point after about a 1,000-foot climb through the spruce, fir, oak, and maple. On the downside of the loop, ash and hemlock trees make up portions of the landscape. Numbered posts are scattered through the trail. They correspond with a pamphlet put out by the U.S. Forest Service that describes the history of the glacial activity and ecology of the area. Lichens, a combination of fungus and algae, grow on the boulders. The plants emit an acid that seeps through the rock, breaking it down, one of the first steps in producing soil. Nature's wrath in the form of a nor'easter is evident in some of the uprooted trees.

The trail leaves Passaconaway Road and comes to a junction after just 0.2 mile. Taking the loop in the clockwise direction brings snowshoers alongside the boulders on a moderate climb. The trail takes a hard right by a large smooth rock face and follows it for a short spell. The trail will then take a hard left into a mixed hardwood and evergreen forest and by some blowdowns.

Wonderful views are yours to experience as the trail advances to an overlook. Look to the south where the weaving Kancamagus Highway and winding Swift River run below. The rocky cone of Mount Chororua is in the distance.

The trail takes a hard left and reenters the woods. At about 1.5 miles a spur trail leads to the ledges. Use good judgment here. It's a short scamper to the ledges with views of the Passaconaway Valley and Mounts Passaconaway and Chororua. Do not get close to the edge of the cliffs. The views are just as fine from a safe vantage point.

> ## Directions at a glance
>
> 0.0 Leave the trailhead for the Boulder Loop Trail.
>
> 0.2 Turn left at the sign saying LEDGES 1.3 MILES.
>
> 1.5 Option exists to turn right for a 0.1-mile snowshoe to a scenic overlook. Or continue 1.3 miles on Boulder Loop Trail.
>
> 2.8 Continue straight at junction with LEDGES sign and return to trailhead.

The main trail curves around the ledges and begins its descent. It's not all downhill at this point, so be prepared for a dip or two before heading back down to the boulders and crossing a small brook. The trail returns to the junction and then back to the road.

How to get there

From Conway travel south on Route 16 about a half mile. Turn right (west) on Route 112, the Kancamagus Highway. Travel 6 miles and turn right on Passaconaway Road. Park in the winter parking area to the right. To reach the trailhead walk over the covered bridge and bear right. The trailhead is on the left, a short way down.

Echo Lake Trail

Echo Lake State Park, North Conway, New Hampshire

Type of trail:	⬭ ▬
Also used by:	Walkers, hikers, snowmobilers
Distance:	1.0-mile loop
Terrain:	A flat trail for families, first-timers, and those looking for a short jaunt
Trail difficulty:	Easiest
Surface quality:	Ungroomed, but packed
Food and facilities:	The facilities at Echo Lake State Park—like water and restrooms—are dormant during winter. Bring all supplies you'll need. Nearby North Conway village is a spot to rent cross-country skis or snowshoes like at Eastern Mountain Sports, Main Street (603–356–5433). After the trip Hooligan's (603–356–6110) on Kearsarge Street is a good dining choice. The Mount Washington Valley Chamber of Commerce (603–356–5701) is a good lodging resource.
Phone numbers:	New Hampshire Division of Parks and Recreation, (603) 271–3556; Carroll County Sheriff's Department, for emergencies only, (800) 552–8960.

The flat Lake Trail in Echo Lake State Park is a pleasant and easy trek along the edge of a frozen lake. The 1.0-mile loop never strays far from water's view and offers both views of distant Mount Kearsarge North and the striking climbing ledges—White Horse and Cathedral. The two ledges, where rock climbers scale granite in summer and fall, and ice climbers play their slippery game in winter, dwarf the small lake.

Popular in summer as a hiking and mountain biking trail, the Lake Trail maintains a certain degree of charm during the snow months. It isn't unusual to come across walkers and their dogs, or even a slow-moving snowmobile, during an outing on the pine-laden trail. Though this trail is used by snowmobiles, snowshoers and skiers can get around this by just circumnavigating the lake when the ice is sufficiently thick and solid.

Directions at a glance

0.0 From the gate by the park, enter the unplowed parking area and head for the gatehouse. At about 200 feet turn right at the gatehouse.

0.1 Turn right on the Lake Trail and follow it around the lake. The trail returns to the unplowed parking lot.

The snow covers the emerald green waters of the lake and its sandy shores. Reminders of summer are everywhere as snowshoers and skiers move past the dormant bathhouses and the snow-covered picnic tables, some propped on their sides. It is the lifeguard chair, bright orange, that is a draw. Climb in and be king of winter's domain in the forest of oak and pine. Straight ahead are the magnificent cliffs called White Horse Ledge. It might take some imagination, but try to spot the horse. To the left are the tips of the Moat Range. You can see the upper section of a hotel built under the ledge, too. Over to the right is the rounded top of Cathedral Ledge. Binoculars are a good idea to try and spot the ice climbers.

Winter hikers often carry snowshoes.

It may be enough for some visitors to just ski or snowshoe across the ice. But the trail is easy and flat. Because of its ease, the excursion is a prime candidate for families with children or newcomers to Nordic skiing and snowshoeing. This trail is particularly enjoyable after a fresh snow. It can harden up some after a famed New England thaw though.

Though the trail can be done in either direction, we go counterclockwise from the beach. Soon, an unsigned trail forks to the right; stay to the left on the Lake Trail, which hugs the shore. The trail rounds the lake and soon a sign points to the Bryce Path on the right. Stay nearest to the shore. Keep an eye on the lifeguard chair. When you are directly across from it, look up to the left and see Mount Kearsarge North. On its top stands a fire tower.

The trail heads away from the shores for a tad and comes to another sign that indicates you are on the Echo Lake Trail. Just after that, a path emerges from the left and leads to the shores of the lake. Stay straight to go to the unplowed parking area and return to your car.

How to get there

From North Conway travel on River Road for approximately 1 mile. Turn right on West Side Road. Turn right a half mile later on Echo Lake Road, following the signs to the park entrance.

Lincoln Woods/Pemi East Side Road Trails

Lincoln, New Hampshire

Type of trail:	▰▰▰ ◉◉◉
Also used by:	Hikers
Distance:	11.0-mile loop
Terrain:	Long but flat ski through New Hampshire wilderness
Trail difficulty:	Easiest, more difficult
Surface quality:	Packed, double tracked
Food and facilities:	Information center, rest rooms, water, and hot chocolate are available at the trailhead. Equipment rentals can be had at Loon's touring center (603–745–8111, ext. 5568). The Lincoln-Woodstock Chamber of Commerce (800–227–4191) has lodging suggestions. Gordi's Fish and Steak House (603–745–6635) is a good après-ski choice. WMNF pass needed at trailhead.
Phone numbers:	Pemigewasset Ranger Station in Plymouth, (603) 536–1310 (It is advised to check in with a ranger at the information center at the trailhead before heading into the Pemigewasset wilderness area or to find out about frozen river crossings.); New Hampshire State Police, (800) 525–5555.

The Lincoln Woods Cross-Country Ski Trails are a mellow winter playground for cross-country skiers and snowshoers. This is one of the most popular winter trail destinations in the White Mountain National Forest. The U.S. Forest Service maintains about 8 miles of trails here, tracking and packing them after a sizeable snowfall. The trails are on opposite sides of the East Branch of the Pemigewasset River, yet both are double tracked with a lane in the middle. Skiers take the tracks. Snowshoers and hikers take the middle.

The Lincoln Woods Trail, on the west side, is an ideal spot for families and first-timers. At its beginning it crosses a 160-foot suspension bridge. The trail then follows a straight line along an old railroad grade to a stone wall at a bridge over Franconia Brook. Along the way the Pemigewasset, with its browns, whites, greens, and brackish colors of winter, offers a soothing vista. The stone wall is a delightful place to stop for lunch. Be prepared for aerial visits from the birds that frequent the area. From here it is a short half-mile jaunt along the Franconia Falls Trail, which parallels the brook to Franconia Falls along an old logging road. Or, take the Black Pond Trail, which first skirts Ice Pond, where block ice was cut during logging days, and then advances to the panorama of Black Pond. Both trails are rated more difficult and are narrow.

START/FINISH

**Lincoln Woods/Pemi
East Side Road Trails**
Scale: 1:48,000 or 1.32" = 1 mile

The Pemi East Side Road Trail, deemed more difficut, runs along the east side of the river on a forest road with a few hills. It ends at a gate that is the boundary for the wilderness area. About 1.0 mile into the trail, look for views of Mount Bond in the distance and then at about the 2.5-mile mark a panorama of Franconia Ridge. A fun option is to take the easy Pine Island Trail, which is about a half mile into East Side. The narrow 0.8-mile trail through red pine bypasses the first hill before rejoining the East Side. There is a spot by the gated boundary to the wilderness area where skiers and shoers are tempted to cross the ice and continue a loop on the Lincoln Woods Trail. This crossing is not recommended.

However there is a way to combine both the Lincoln Woods and East Side Trails for an 11.0-mile backcountry loop suitable for better skiers and snowshoers. Follow the East Side Trail until you reach the gated boundary of the wilderness area and continue past the gate. The trail is now called the Wilderness Trail, and it is not maintained by the Forest Service. Instead the tracks are made by skiers passing through.

Directions at a glance

0.0 Follow the Pemi East Side Road Trail.

2.9 Continue straight past gate to wilderness area.

5.0 Bear left at signed junction with Cedar Brook Trail.

5.5 Cross suspension bridge and make left on Wilderness Trail, which becomes Lincoln Woods Trail.

11.0 Turn left at suspension bridge. First left, then the first right leads back to information center and parking area.

There are several vantage points from which to view the river, but then the trail heads east and away from the rushing waters. It is on this stretch that several small water run-offs must be crossed. The amount of snow will determine the width of the crossings. The trail crosses Cedar Brook and soon climbs steeply to a junction with the signed Cedar Brook Trail. From there it is about a half mile to a suspension bridge that spans the river. The west side of the river is much flatter and is a virtual straight shot all the way along a railroad grade. In less than 1.0 mile, you pass an old trestle across a bridge. There is a slight dip before the bridge. The trail then passes a junction with the Bondcliff Trail. When reaching the bridge over Franconia Brook, there is only about 2.8 miles left. An option exists here for side excursions to the falls and Black Pond. The trail will leave the river's edge, heading away from it. Pass a campsite, its status in flux due to overuse. The trail returns with river views after it passes the Osseo Trail. Finally the loop ends after crossing the suspension bridge that leads back to the trailhead.

How to get there

The Lincoln Woods Cross-Country Ski Trails are located about 5 miles east of I–93, exit 32, on the Kancamagus Highway (Route 112).

North End Loop

The Nordic Center at Waterville Valley, New Hampshire

Type of trail:	▬▬ ◄ ⬭
Distance:	Nearly 3.0 miles
Terrain:	Backcountry feeling not too far from civilization with stellar mountain panoramas on occasion
Trail difficulty:	Easiest for snowshoers, more difficult for skiers
Surface quality:	Double tracked with a skate lane
Food and facilities:	The Nordic Center is filled with options. Both snowshoe and cross-country rentals are available, a retail shop offers supplies and equipment, and you can sign up for lessons (skate and classical). Ice skating can be had, too. Throughout the season there are special events as well as guided ski and snowshoe tours beginning from the Town Square. Be sure to stop at the center to purchase a trail pass or get the latest word on conditions and the weather. The square also has restaurants featuring anything from pizza to crab cakes for that post-adventure craving. Last minute snacks are also available. For those heading home, consider a stop at the Mad River Tavern on Route 49, about 10 miles from the ski center. If it's Wednesday it's Mexican night. Bueno. Lodging opportunities are varied as well. The Golden Eagle Lodge (800–910–4499) is convenient to the square. There is no water available during the outing. Picnic tables are found throughout, and toilet facilities are at the trailhead.
Phone numbers:	The Nordic Center at Waterville Valley is (603) 236–4666. For central reservations in Waterville, call (800) GO VALLEY.

Smack in the White Mountains, the trails at Waterville Valley can be a jumping-off point for beginners who just want to go around a still, frozen pond, or a challenging series of hairpin turns for the speediest of skate skiers. No matter what the level of the adventurer, the trails find solitude in the woods with chance sightings of moose and panoramic mountain views of New Hampshire's 4,000-foot peaks.

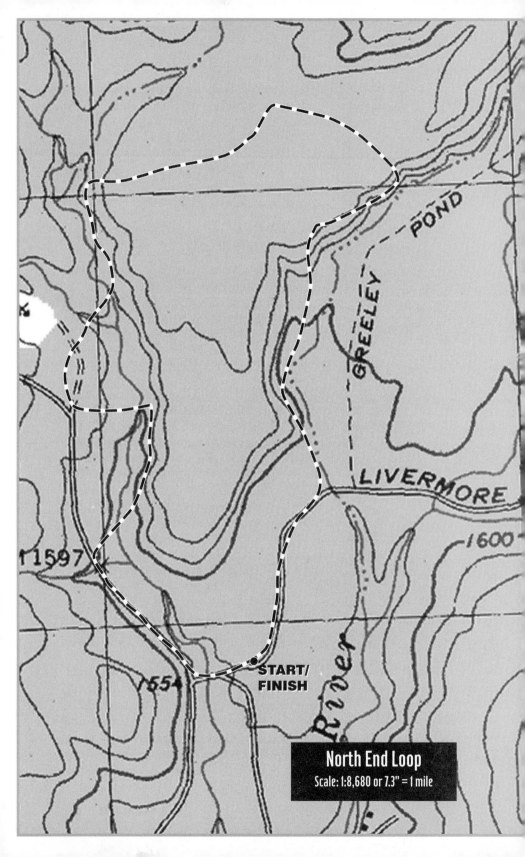

GREELEY POND

LIVERMORE

1600

11597

1554

River

START/
FINISH

North End Loop
Scale: 1:8,680 or 7.3" = 1 mile

Waterville is a four-season resort that has hosted everything from World Cup ski races to world-class concerts. Whether it's a weeklong family vacation or a day trip, there are about 40 miles of groomed trails and nearly 20 miles of backcountry to explore. The Nordic network opened in 1973 and now allows snowshoers on all the trails. Groomed trails have two tracked lanes separated by a 10-foot-wide skate lane.

The heart of the network is in Town Square, the village hub. The system is broken into two quadrants, north and south. Though south has some easier trails like the popular Pond Loop around Corcoran's Pond, expert skiers can also find a challenge on the Criterion, a trail specifically laid out for racing. It's evenly divided with ups, downs, and flats. Snowshoers tend to like the Village Trail, which parallels both Snows Brook and the Mad River.

The north end, according to Nordic Director Mike Seeger, is prime habitat for wildlife. A former forest ranger, Seeger and mountain guide Walt Stockwell were quick to point to snowshoe hare and moose tracks during an early season jaunt. Popular with upper-level skiers is the Cascade Brook Loop with its series of S-curves. But entry-level snowshoers and skiers who can sustain a strong snowplow will want to try the nearly 3-mile-long North End Loop, a series of trails with vistas of frosty Mount Tecumseh and its alpine trails, Osceola, Tripyramid, Snow's Mountain, and the Sandwich Range.

Directions at a glance

0.0   Leave the trailhead by heading over bridge and Tecumseh Brook. Turn right on Osceola Trail (also Tripoli Road).

0.5   Bear right on Osceola Trail through Osceola Vista Campground.

0.6   Bear left via Bob's Lookout Trail which loops through Osceola Vista Campground. Rejoin the Osceola Trail, bearing left after crossing a bridge.

1.0   Turn right on Moose Run and Wicked Easy Trails.

1.6   Stay straight on Wicked Easy Trail.

2.3   Turn left on Moose Run.

2.4   Turn left on Redfeather Trail.

2.6   Turn right on Livermore Road.

2.8   Turn right into parking area.

Well-marked with frequent maps, the circuit gets under way on the wide Osceola Trail. The trail is really on Tripoli Road, a dirt and paved road that cuts through the Mad River Notch and is open in summer. But in winter, it becomes a white, wide path leading to the dormant Osceola Vista Campground in the White Mountain National Forest. Amid the picnic tables and snow-covered fire rings is a knoll called Bob's Lookout. From it, look out at the ring of the White Mountains.

The trail with its pending yellow birch and evergreens stays in the shelter of the forest, a protective force from cold winter winds. Easy bridge crossings over chilled brooks are part of the adventure, as are the winter views of the mountains. Osceola Trail hands off to a couple of easy trails, Moose Run and Wicked Easy. Wicked Easy hands off to Moose Run, which has a conveniently placed picnic table. Now comes the rolling Redfeather Trail. It's a real hoot for snowshoers as it bears right and plunges to a beaver pond. Skiers should like being in that flying V snowplow to wind down. There are glimpses of Tripyramid through the naked trees. After the narrow chute, it's back to the wide flats of Livermore Road, though better free-heelers might want to snake back to the parking area via the Deep Woods Trail. However, both lead back to the starting point of a civilized winter experience.

Skiers play on the trails at Waterville Valley.

How to get there

From I–93, take exit 28 and travel 11 miles on Route 49 to Waterville Valley. Turn left on Village Road to the Nordic Center in Town Square.

To reach the Depot Camp trailhead from the Nordic Center, leave Town Square on Village Road and travel 0.1 mile to stop sign and Valley Road. Turn left on Valley Road and drive 0.1 mile to turn right on Valley Road. Travel 0.3 mile and turn left on West Branch Road. Drive 0.8 mile and turn right into Depot Camp trailhead. Walk out of the parking lot and bear right across a bridge. The Osceola Trail, which is also Tripoli Road, leaves right.

Around-Lonesome-Lake Trail

Franconia, New Hampshire

Type of trail:	⬭
Also used by:	Hikers
Distance:	3.2 miles
Terrain:	Flat to hilly, delightful snowshoe to frozen lake with alpine vistas
Trail difficulty:	More difficult
Surface quality:	Ungroomed
Food and facilities:	No facilities, except for a pay phone, exist at the trailhead. Winter camping without facilities is available at the Lafayette Place Campground (603–271–3556). Close by is the Cannon Mountain ski area, at exit 2 off Franconia Notch Parkway (603–823–5563). Snowshoe rentals (603–823–5563) are available at Cannon Mountain, as are rest rooms and a cafeteria. Also of note: You can take a round-trip tram ride to the top of the 4,100-foot peak to snowshoe the 0.5-mile Rim Trail. Tickets are available at the base lodge. The New England Ski Museum (603–823–7177) is next to the base area and well worth a visit. After the trip consider Chieng Gardens (603–745–8612) on Main Street in Lincoln.
Phone numbers:	Franconia Notch State Park, (603) 823–5563; New Hampshire State Police, (800) 525–5555.

One of the finest snowshoe trips in the White Mountains is a trek to the serene shores of Lonesome Lake in Franconia Notch State Park. The lake sits in a basin under the twin peaks of 4,293-foot North Kinsman and the 4,358-foot South Kinsman. But the prize in this jaunt is the dazzling beauty of the Franconia Ridge. The snow-choked ravines are like fingers between the crusty ridges. During a day of sunshine, the combination of the wind-drifted snow on the frozen lake, the Kinsman pair, and the Franconias are like a perfectly executed oil painting. One must reach out and touch to see if it is real.

The snowshoe trek begins at the well-signed Lonesome Lake Trailhead. The trailhead is also used by snowmobilers riding the paved bike path through the notch. Begin by taking a hand-railed footbridge over the Pemigewasset, crossing the Pemi Trail, and passing through the sleeping campground along the yellow-blazed trail.

After leaving the campground the trail begins a long, moderate climb of 1,000 feet through the hardwoods over a series of switchbacks. Cross

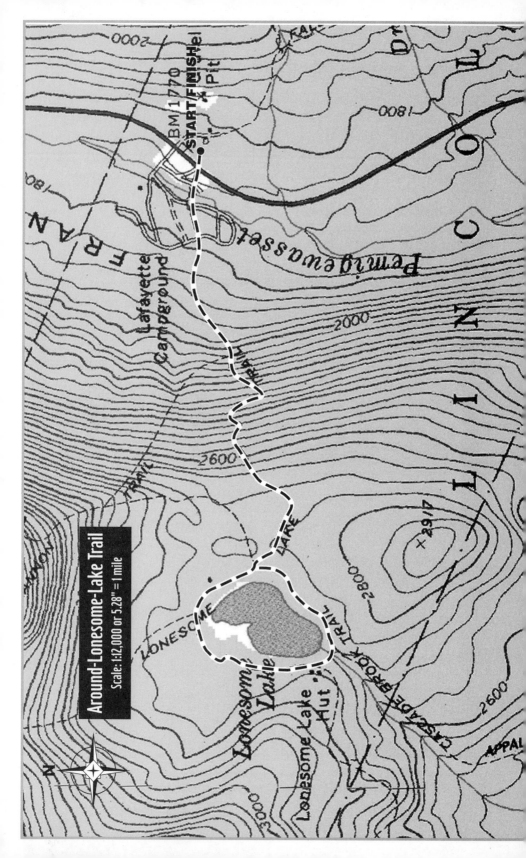

Around-Lonesome-Lake Trail
Scale: 1:12,000 or 5.28" = 1 mile

BM 1770
START/FINISH
el. Pit

Lafayette
Campground

FRAN

Pemigewasset

LINCOL

2000

2600

2000

LONESOME

2917

2800

LAKE

Lonesome
Lake

CASCADE BROOK TRAIL

TRAIL

CANNON

2800

Lonesome Lake
Hut

3000

2600

APPAL

N

A skier enjoys the solitude.

a small wooden bridge over a brook at about 0.3 mile and then one more bridge shortly thereafter. At about 0.4 mile the Hi-Cannon Trail enters right. For the most part the trail follows an old bridle path. As it winds its way up the ridge, it is sometimes narrow. While resting, look behind through the birch to see the sparkling Franconia Range.

The forest changes as the ascent continues. Soon evergreens reign. The sounds of the traffic rolling along the road below are a memory. Quiet takes over during a short dip to a junction near the edge of the lake. It is here that the Cascade Trail heads left and the Dodge Cut-off goes right. A small path at the junction heads down to the eastern shore of the lake.

Now you must make a decision. If it is sunny and the lake is suffi-cently frozen, it is a pleasure to snowshoe directly across the lake to the Appalachian Mountain Club's Lonesome Lake Hut on the southwest shores. Look closely and you will see the cabins from the eastern shore.

However there is an option of taking the Around-Lonesome-Lake Trail, an 0.8-mile loop. The trail is flat and is made up of a number of dif-ferent trails. The downside of this trail is that portions of it pass through boggy sections that are traversed by narrow log bridges.

Take the Around-Lonesome-Lake Trail by making a left on the Lone-some Lake Trail. The blue-blazed trail nears the shore, and after 0.2 mile, the Around-Lonesome-Lake Trail bears right. After that the Fishin' Jimmy Trail (part of the Appalachian Trail) enters. Take it and bear right, cross a log bridge over a stream, and start to look for the snow-covered sandy beach.

Across the water is an awe-inspiring view—the Franconias. From left to right there are Mount Lafayette at 5,260 feet, Mount Lincoln at 5,089 feet, and Little Haystack Mountain at 4,760 feet.

At the beach there is a sign pointing to the Lonesome Lake Hut. The hut, at about 2,760 feet, was built in 1964 and is open from May to October.

These shores are an ideal lunch spot. The Fishin' Jimmy Trail continues to round the lake. It crosses the brooks and bogs of the western shore at fine vantage points. It also crosses numerous narrow bridges.

Bear right on the Cascade Brook Trail as the path reenters the woods and then meets the junction of the Lonesome Lake Trail again. You have been here before. Take one last look at the lake before heading left on the Lonesome Lake Trail.

The descent doesn't appear to be as long as the ascent. Try to snatch a glimpse of the Franconias on the way down if you can stop looking at your feet. The familiar trail snakes downward, through the campground and back to the parking area.

How to get there

From the south exit the Franconia Notch State Parkway at the sign for Lafayette Place Campground. Turn left in the parking area. An underpass will lead to the other side of the road and the trailhead.

From the north exit the Franconia Notch State Parkway at the sign for Lafayette Place Campground. The trailhead is opposite the brown visitor center.

Directions at a glance

0.0 Leave via Lonesome Lake Trail.

0.4 Hi-Cannon Trail enters from the right.

1.2 There is a four-way junction at the pond's edge. Turn left for Around-Lonesome-Lake Trail via Cascade Brook Trail.

1.4 Bear left on Around-Lonesome-Lake Trail.

1.6 Continue straight on Fishin' Jimmy Trail.

1.8 Bear right on Cascade Brook Trail.

2.0 Turn left on Lonesome Lake Trail and descend the 1.2-mile trail to the parking area.

Lower Nanamocomuck Ski Trail

Albany, New Hampshire

Type of trail:	━━━ ▰▰▰
Also used by:	Hikers
Distance:	6.9 miles one way
Terrain:	Flat and rolling classic ski in the White Mountains along the Swift River
Trail difficulty:	Easiest to more difficult
Surface quality:	Ungroomed, skier tracked
Food and facilities:	Toilets are available at trail's end in the Albany Covered Bridge parking area, but food and water are not. This trail system is not patrolled by the U.S. Forest Service. After the ski stop in Conway at Cafe Noche (603–447–5050). Rentals are available in North Conway at Eastern Mountain Sports (603–356–5433). The Mount Washington Valley Chamber of Commerce (603–356–3171) can suggest lodging. WMNF pass needed.
Phone numbers:	For the latest trail conditions, the Saco Ranger station, (603) 447–5448; for emergencies, the Carroll County Sheriff's Department, (800) 552–8960.

The Lower Nanamocomuck Ski Trail parallels the boulder-strewn Swift River, affording skiers and snowshoers miles of opportunities for adventure. This is a gem of a trail because there are an incredible number of vistas and trail options. The Swift River itself is stunning. The trail runs along its length for a good portion of the route, cuts back into the forest, then comes back to water's edge. At Rocky Gorge skiers and shoers can choose to visit the quiet, frozen shores of Falls Pond and gaze up among the spruce and pine to see Bear Mountain, or they can cross a bridge to see the roiling waters of the gorge against walls of granite. (Remove your skis before entering the Rocky Gorge area because there are steps and the bridge crossing for those who go to view the rushing waters.) There is one more option here. The Lovequist Loop, a 0.7-mile trail around Falls Pond, is an ideal spot for snowshoeing in either direction because it swings between forest and shore.

Along the trail there are a few loop options to consider as well. The Wenonah and Wenunchus Ski Trails—spurs off the Lower Nanamocomuck—can be skied in either direction. Here are grueling climbs and exhilarating downhills for the more advanced skier. These two trails later rejoin the Lower Nanamocomuck.

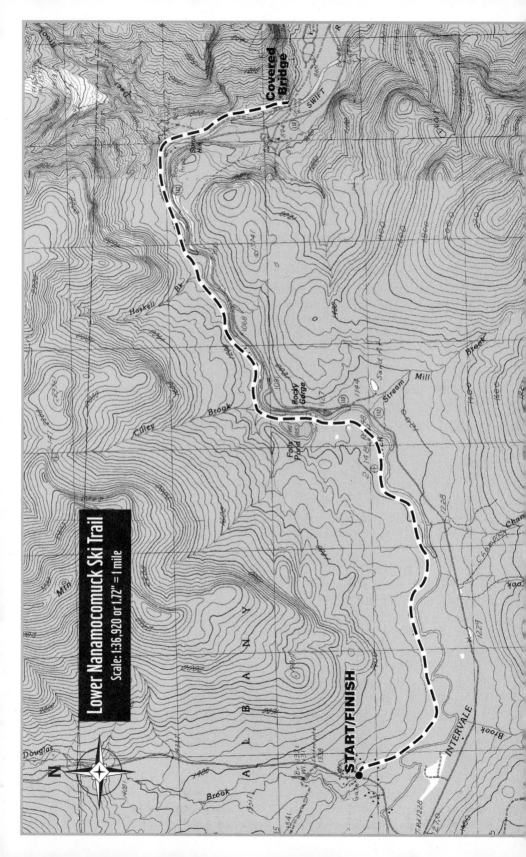

Lower Nanamocomuck Ski Trail
Scale: 1:36,920 or 1.72" = 1 mile

Covered Bridge

START/FINISH

N

Now a few words about all those Native American names. Many of the peaks in the White Mountains are named after the Indians who once lived in the area. Kancamagus, "The Fearless One," was chief of the Penacook tribe in the 1680s. His father was Nanamocomuck. Wenonah happened to be the daughter of Chocorua and the wife of Wonalancet, while Wenunchus was the daughter of Passaconway and sister of Nanamocomuck. Don't worry, there isn't a quiz.

Though the Lower Nanamocomuck is rated easiest, it should not be attempted by beginner skiers who are out for a first outing. There are sections where snow-plow and herringbone or sidestepping skills are necessary. As for snowshoers, please try to stay off the ski tracks.

Throughout the journey the trail is marked with blue, plastic diamonds. There are nearly a dozen bridge crossings. Just try not to catch a pole in the gaps between the planks. Many signs tick off the miles, alerting trail-users to where they are. This journey is from east to west, dropping in elevation from 1,340 feet on Bear Notch Road to 880 feet by the covered bridge.

The initial section of the trail is a bit bumpy and narrow through the evergreens. Depending on the amount of snowfall, there are some wet areas that you'll traverse. But shortly thereafter you'll encounter the first of many downhill bursts. The trail eventually makes its way to the banks of the Swift River, where it rolls along its edges. The snow attempts to cover examples of the erosion that has taken place over the years. After about 2.5 miles—past several spots at which to gaze and ponder—the trail takes a hard left and begins a twisting climb up through the forest before submitting to gravity. The trail descends to a junction with the Wenonah Trail. Now head to Rocky Gorge, more than midway on this jaunt. It is here that skiers climb rather steeply only to have to ride down again. These hills might prove too much for some beginner skiers. Take off your skis, particularly if conditions are icy, and walk to where you can

Directions at a glance

0.0 Leave the parking area on the Lower Nanamocomuck Trail. There is a sign.

0.7 Turn right on the Lower Nanamocomuck. The Paugus Trail enters from the left.

3.5 Bear right on the Lower Nanamocomuck at the junction of the Wenonah Trail.

4.3 Bear right on the Lower Nanamocomuck toward the Covered Bridge campground. The Wenunchus Trail enters from the left.

6.0 Turn right on the Lower Nanamocomuck.

6.2 Turn right on Deer Brook Road (Forest Road 28), part of the Lower Nanamocomuck.

6.9 Turn right, go across the bridge to the parking area.

The Albany Covered Bridge is the ending point for a pleasant ski along the Lower Nanamocomuck Ski Trail.

spot Falls Pond and Rocky Gorge. Down the steps is the churning water. To the left is the peaceful shore. The loop around the pond is closed to cross-country skiers, but snowshoers can circumnavigate the shores.

The Lower Nanamocomuck continues with a few more dips. The first descent after Rocky Gorge has a bridge near its bottom. It is easy to cross. Just be forewarned. The trail flattens out some and finds the Swift again as the Wenunchus Trail enters as an option.

Tiny drainages present some narrow crossings along the river bank, depending on the amount of snow. Use good judgment.

Once again the trail leaves water's edge to climb a bit into the forest. But it is now less than 2.0 miles to the covered bridge. Look down on the waters of the Swift after climbing a ridge. The route heads gently down to a junction where a wide forest road awaits. On Deer Brook Road a portion of the Lower Nanamocomuck, skiers are treated to something special. The last 1.0 mile of this tour is wide and an easy sloping downhill. Stop to admire the waters and vistas. When you spot the Albany covered bridge (1858), you are near trail's end. Head across the brown bridge to the parking area.

How to get there

To reach the Lower Nanamocomuck Ski Trailhead on Bear Notch Road in Bartlett, New Hampshire, travel on the Kancamagus Highway (Route 112) approximately 12 miles west of Conway and turn right on Bear Notch Road. Travel 1 mile and park in the plowed area. For the Albany

Covered Bridge parking area, travel 6 miles west on the Kancamagus Highway from Conway and turn right on Passaconway Road.

The middle of the trail can be accessed via Rocky Gorge, which is about 8.5 miles west of Conway on the Kancamagus Highway. Parking is available at the east end of the Rocky Gorge Service Road. Snowshoers looking to walk the Lovequist Loop will begin here.

We suggest parking one car on Bear Notch Road and another at the covered bridge for this tour.

Old Bridle Path
Holderness, New Hampshire

Type of trail:	(icon)
Also used by:	Hikers
Distance:	0.9 mile one way; 1.8 miles round-trip
Terrain:	Easy trek to frozen Squam Lake views
Trail difficulty:	Easiest
Surface quality:	Ungroomed
Food and facilities:	There are no facilities. Both Meredith and Holderness have stores for last minute items. Try Guiseppe's (603–279–3313) at the Mill Falls Marketplace in Meredith for a pizza. The Meredith Inn at Mill Falls (603–279–7006) offers overnighters a place to stay in nearby Meredith. Rentals are available in Meredith at Sports and Marine Parafunalia (603–279–8077).
Phone numbers:	Squam Lakes Association, (603) 968–7336; Holderness Police for emergencies, (603) 968–3333.

The trip up West Rattlesnake by way of the Old Bridle Path is one of the best snowshoes in New Hampshire's Lakes Region. At 0.9 mile one way, this short and easy journey will reward you with its beautiful views. Beginners and families will no doubt be attracted to the path because of its ease. Those who look for more challenging terrain should not overlook this jaunt and shortchange themselves. On a day when you just want to get out for a couple of hours, or have slept in a bit, this is the one to choose.

The trail, an old carriage road, is blazed in yellow and is maintained by the Squam Lakes Association. The association says the trail is the most heavily used in the area. Once you're up at the 1,260-foot summit,

N

Old Bridle Path
Scale: 1:12,000 or 5.28" = 1 mile

TRAIL

START/FINISH

BRIDLE

Cem

UNDERCUT

800 PATH

PATH

The

Ra

RIDGE

RAMSEY TR

PASTURE

1000

COL TR

TR

RA

800

600

Bk

Cem

Bk

600

600

Bennett

Rockywold

the views south and west of Big Squam Lake and the surrounding mountains are nothing short of spectacular.

West Rattlesnake and neighboring East Rattlesnake are two small mountains on the northern edge of Squam Lake. While ascending the Old Bridle Path, and certainly during the descent, the silhouette of the Squam Range with Mounts Morgan and Percival is unmistakable.

From the top and the open ledges, look down some 500 feet on the lake's many coves and islands. The state's largest lake, Winnipesaukee, is out in the distance. The peak with the fire tower is 2,384-foot Mount Belknap in Gilford. The flat slabs of rock at the summit are ideal spots for a lunch and a wonderful place to gather inspiration.

Directions at a glance

0.0 Leave the trailhead for the Old Bridle Path to West Rattlesnake and travel 0.9 mile.

0.9 Reach summit.

Return the same way via Old Bridle Path to trailhead.

Squam Lake may bring back memories for snowshoers of a certain age. It was on those waters that the movie *On Golden Pond,* featuring Katharine Hepburn, Henry Fonda, and Jane Fonda, was filmed, bringing notoriety to the area.

The Old Bridle Path is very easy to follow. From the parking lot cross Route 113 and turn right. It's a couple of hundred feet to the signed trailhead. The wide path is a gradual climb, with several flat spots for those who need a breather. Children will enjoy looking for trees that have been used as a construction zone by the pileated woodpecker.

There are those who might wish they had brought their skis for a trip downhill from the summit. The Squam Lakes Association does not recommend this trail for skiing.

How to get there

From Meredith travel on Routes 3 north/25 west from the traffic lights at the junction with Route 16. Drive 8.0 miles and turn right on Route 113 in Holderness heading east. At 5.6 miles turn left into the trail parking area. The trail is across the street and to the right.

Ellis River Trail

Jackson, New Hampshire

Type of trail:	▬▬ ◄
Distance:	15.5 miles
Terrain:	Long, flat to hilly journey along a White Mountain favorite
Trail difficulty:	Easiest to most difficult
Surface quality:	Single tracked, double tracked, skating portions
Food and facilities:	Instruction, rentals, rest rooms, trail passes, wax room, and advice are available from the Jackson Ski Touring Foundation headquarters. A warm-ing hut is located on the Ellis River Trail. For skiing the Ellis River Trail one way, shuttle service is available on weekends from its terminus at the Dana Place Inn. Spotting a second car at the inn will suffice during mid-week. For after-ski meals, there are a number of inns and restaurants in Jackson, including the Red Fox Pub (603–383–6659) and Jackson Bistro (603–383–6633). The Jackson Chamber of Commerce (603–383–9356) is a good lodging resource.
Phone numbers:	Jackson Ski Touring Foundation, (603) 383–9355 or (800) XC–SNOWS.

Sometimes it's just hard to choose a trail to ski at a cross-country ski center. That can happen in Jackson, New Hampshire. When it does, try this long loop, which features three of the system's trails—Ellis River, High Water, and the Hall.

The Ellis River Trail is a favorite among White Mountain trails. The trail runs through evergreens and hardwoods close to the waters of the west bank of the Ellis River, its 4.5-mile length terminating at a warm inn. The trail is like a park—well groomed and civilized. The Ellis River Trail has one-way sections, offering north and south corridors. Each direction yields a different experience.

The Hall Trail runs nearly 7.5 miles and offers both a challenge and vistas of Mount Isolation and Wildcat Mountain as it crests Popple Mountain. Though the climb is long, so is the winding and exhilarating downhill. The views of the eastern range of the Presidentials from clear-cuts are worth the trip. Add a couple of connector trails to this exciting downhill and you have the makings of a day's outing.

The trails are part of the Jackson Ski Touring Foundation, a nonprofit membership organization formed in 1972 to maintain cross-country ski trails in and around beautiful Jackson village. The system uses the land of

Gliding over a bridge, this cross-country skier crosses a rocky stream.

seventy-five private landowners and town municipal land and operates in the White Mountain National Forest through a special-use permit. The network of sixty-five trails covers 100 miles and has been host to a number of world-class events, including the 1990 World Nordic Disabled Championships, the 1985 International Relays, and the 1984 and 1995 NCAA College Championships. There are also a few miles of snowshoe trails.

From ski headquarters, ski west across the flats of an open field, and over a covered bridge. A tunnel provides access to the far side of Route 16 before the route crosses Green Hill Road and the trail along the Ellis River begins. The trail has a few quick dips and hills, with wide bridge crossings. A warming hut comes about a mile from Green Hill Road.

Several loop options and short side trips make themselves available, like a ski to Winniweta Falls, Gray's Field, and the old Dollof Farm site. The signs are well placed, and it is no effort to follow them.

Directions at a glance

0.0 Leave the touring center on the Wentworth Trail, eventually crossing a covered bridge and using a tunnel under Route 16.

0.7 Take off the skis, cross Green Hill Road, and continue right on the Ellis River Trail.

5.2 Turn left on the High Water Trail.

6.2 Turn left on the Hall Trail.

13.7 Turn right on the Ellis River Trail.

15.0 Cross Green Hill Road, turn left on the Wentworth Trail, and follow it a half mile back to the touring center.

The Ellis River Trail leads to the High Water Trail, a more difficult trail that darts in and along the river bank for about a mile before reaching the Rocky Branch parking lot. It is here that the Hall Trail begins.

Prepare to climb. The long climb up the Hall to Popple Mountain passes by clear-cuts with views of 4,005-foot-high Mount Isolation looming in the distance. After cresting the summit there is a quick descent and hairpin turn just before the trail passes Maple Mountain Loop (a 2.0-mile side trail). The long, wondrous downhill continues past a scenic vista you can access by a short side trail. Be sure to take it to see the eastern slope mountains, including Black, Doublehead, Kearsarge, Sable, Chandler, Tin, Thorn, and others. Just before the trail rejoins the Ellis River Trail, there is a steep and fast drop, which passes through the scenic wildlife area, Gray's Field, before heading back to the flats of the village.

How to get there

The Jackson Ski Touring Foundation is located on Route 16A in the village of Jackson. Head north on Route 16 from the Glen intersection of Routes 16 and 302. Travel 2.5 miles to Jackson, passing the covered bridge, and turn right on Route 16A by a gas station. The touring center is one-third of a mile down on the right. If traveling from the north, take Route 16 south from Gorham, New Hampshire, 20 miles through Pinkham Notch to Jackson.

Upper Saco River Loop

Bartlett, New Hampshire

Type of trail: ▬▬ ＜ ●

Distance: 4.7 miles

Terrain: Just a few hills for a Saco River ski

Trail difficulty: More difficult

Surface quality: Groomed, single tracked

Food and facilities: Rentals (cross-country and snowshoes), lessons, a wax room, and snacks—including hot soups—are available at the touring center. After the ski try the Bear Notch Deli in Bartlett, (603) 374–2445. The Country Inn of Bartlett (603–374–2353) is nearby for an overnight.

Phone numbers: Bear Notch Ski Touring Center, (603) 374–2277.

Back in 1994 a couple of homegrown Bartlett brothers—Doug and John Garland—decided to start a cross-country ski area on the family property, which bordered the Saco River and White Mountain National Forest. During the first year the fledgling area took only donations. Now, the laidback, low-key network has grown to some 40 miles of ski trails, which allow snowshoers, too. About 10 miles of trails are dedicated to snowshoeing.

The small touring center is beyond rustic. It is shining backwoods scenic and simple. Walk into the woodsy center and maybe there will be bread baking in the corner. Check out the pool table that has denim pants legs as pockets. The beams in the center haven't had their bark removed.

It is the western network with trails meandering along the rocky-bottomed Saco River that is the attraction for many beginners and intermediates. Along the rolling waters the trails look straight up at Crawford Notch to the west and the slopes of the Attitash Bear Peak ski area to the east. The fourteenth highest peak in New Hampshire, 4,680-foot Mount Carrigain, provides a snow-capped backdrop against the clear, wild river.

The Saco isn't the only waterway playing a part in the show that is the Upper Saco River Loop. The Albany Brook flows down to a small waterfall by a screened-in summer cabin. Skiers and snowshoers cross a small bridge by the falls and can stop to admire the scenery.

For the most part the trails at the Bear Notch Ski Touring Center are not named but numbered and circled with a snowflake. The Upper Saco River Loop is largely agreeable to beginner skiers, but its sharp, spirited hills might cause them to seek an alternate route to the flats of the Saco.

The loop is a collection of trails that wind and weave their way through the woods, flats, and hills of the network. The trail that parallels the Saco, number 16, also affords skiers and snowshoers the opportunity for two miniloops, keeping them within the sights of the clear, white-topped waters.

From the touring center, trail 10 winds through the woods to a road crossing. Once on the other side, trail 11 enters left, and here the path rolls across two stream crossings, followed by a short, steep downhill. Trail 12 is a flat experience, crossing over the train tracks that follow the river. It is when rounding a corner on trail 16 that the Saco comes into view. The trail goes oh-so-close to the water's edge, sometimes giving the impression that you are skiing on a beach or peninsula. Trails 17 (look for beaver dams) and 13 are flat connectors, with trail 13 providing a turn just after crossing a railroad bridge. Though the loop continues through the maples with trails 20 and 21, those seeking more river frontage views should take trail 30 from trail 13 for a flat 1.5-mile ski to River Road, before turning back.

Back across the road the loop's final leg is on trail 2 by the waterfall. It leads to trail 1 and a footbridge back to the touring center.

Directions at a glance

0.0 Leave the back of the touring center on trail 10.

0.3 Take off skis to cross road, then turn left on trail 11.

1.5 Turn left on trail 12.

1.7 Bear left on trail 16, which has two loops. Ski each one clockwise. After the second, return along trail 16 to first loop. Bear to the left on trail 16.

3.0 Turn left on trail 12.

3.2 Turn left on trail 17.

3.7 Turn left on trail 13. As an option bear left on trail 30 for a round-trip 3.0-mile ski to River Road and back.

4.0 Turn right on trail 21.

4.2 Bear right on trail 20.

4.3 Take off·skis to cross road and continue straight on trail 2.

4.5 Turn right on trail 1 and follow it 0.2 mile back to the touring center.

How to get there
From North Conway travel west 12 miles on Route 302 through Bartlett.

Cardigan Loop
Alexandria, New Hampshire

Type of trail:	⬭ ▬
Also used by:	Winter hikers, backcountry skiers
Distance:	3.7 miles
Terrain:	A hilly snowshoe to the rocky dome of a popular Granite State Peak
Trail difficulty:	More difficult for snowshoers, most difficult for skiers
Surface quality:	Ungroomed
Food and facilities:	Portable toilets outside the Appalachian Mountain Club's Cardigan Lodge are available to day users. Water bottles can be topped off as well. Pick food up in Bristol at the market or convenience stores. Afterward, try the Bristol House of Pizza (603–744–3765) on Route 3A. The Cardigan Lodge (603–744–8011) has overnight facilities.
Phone numbers:	Appalachian Mountain Club's Cardigan Lodge, (603) 744–8011, for trail information.

Mount Cardigan, or "Old Baldy," is one of those mountains special to followers of various activities. For the hiker the relatively easy ascent to the rocky dome affords excellent views along the open-faced slab ledges. Cardigan's 3,121-foot summit is a goal of many a beginner hiker.

For the backcountry skier Cardigan provides a sense of belonging and history. Before the modern ski lift transported skiers to the top of a mountain for a run down groomed corduroy boulevards, rugged Appalachian Mountain Club volunteers in the early 1930s had transformed a barn on the east side of Cardigan into what evolved into the Cardigan Lodge, built in 1939. They cut ski trails, the first being the 1.0-mile-long Duke's Run down the north peak of Cardigan, called Firescrew. Over the years the Civilian Conservation Corps stepped in to cut other trails, like the 0.75-mile Alexandria Ski Trail named after the neighboring small town.

Snowshoers and skiers now head to Cardigan to tackle the small network of trails mostly designed for the better backcountry skier. Novice

Directions at a glance

0.0 Leave the parking area on the Holt Trail.

1.1 Arrive at Grand Junction. Turn left on Cathedral Forest Trail.

1.7 Turn right on the Clark Trail.

1.9 Turn right on the Alexandria Ski Trail.

2.6 Bear right on the Holt Trail 1.1 miles back to the parking area.

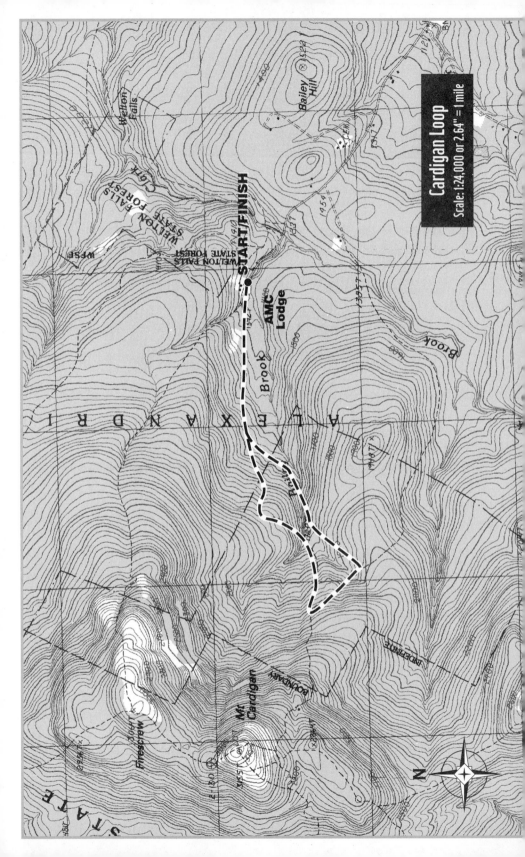

Cardigan Loop
Scale: 1:24,000 or 2.64" = 1 mile

skiers will find little choice, while strong intermediate skiers may find a challenge.

As snowshoeing gains in popularity, a trip up Cardigan could become a rite of passage as well. However the exposed ledges can be exposed to severe wind and become extremely icy. Your trip does not go to the summit though. Instead it combines several popular hiking trails, which lead to a stunning outcrop of views, including the cliffs of Firescrew and the swelling hills of southern New Hampshire. Though many skiers just ski up and then down the Alexandria Ski Trail, this loop affords the opportunity to combine a snowshoe and ski experience.

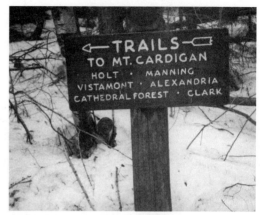

Skiers and snowshoers can choose from many options at the base of Mount Cardigan.

Starting at the lodge the Holt Trail is a wide, gravel road through the low hardwood forest. Travel past a snow-covered picnic area and pass a boundary into the Mount Cardigan State Park. Bailey Brook rushes by as the trail ascends gently to the Bailey Brook Bridge.

Cross the bridge and the trail ascends more moderately until it comes to an area of commingling trails called Grand Junction. From here those on skis can pick up the Alexandria Ski Trail for the up-and-down experience. Snowshoers are not allowed on the ski trail.

By turning left on the yellow-blazed Cathedral Forest Trail, snowshoers will be traveling on the easiest eastern route up Cardigan—several switchbacks through a section of the forest damaged by the ice storm in January 1998.

The Cathedral Forest hands off to the Clark Trail through a grove of evergreens. You travel on more switchbacks until the trail joins up with the Alexandria Ski Trail near a spot called PJ Ledge. From this vantage point enjoy the views. Those seeking the summit experience can turn left and head up 0.7 mile on the Clark Trail, crossing exposed slab areas and passing two cabins.

For the most part the expert Alexandria Ski Trail is about 20 feet wide, but it is narrower at the onset. It is best tackled by expert backcountry skiers after about a foot of fresh powder. Expect steep drops (20 to 25 degrees) and twists as it winds its way back down to Grand Junction. Here you can cross the Bailey Brook Bridge again. The Holt Trail leads you back to the parking area.

How to get there

From I–93 take exit 23 and travel on Route 104 west to Bristol. In Bristol take Route 3A north about 2.5 miles. Turn left at the blinking light onto West Shore Road. In about 2.0 miles the road will bear to the right. Go straight. In about 1.0 mile a sign will point to the AMC. Take that right on Fawler River Road. Some 3.3 miles later another sign will point to the AMC. That's a left on Brook Road. Follow Brook Road and make a right on Shem Valley Road—where there is another AMC sign. Follow the road to the lodge and trailhead. Four-wheel drive is suggested for the final stretch on Shem Valley Road to the lodge.

Cascade Loop

Norsk Cross-Country Ski Center, New London, New Hampshire

Type of trail:	▬▬ ◄
Distance:	6.5 miles
Terrain:	Mount Kearsarge stands guard over gentle woodlands
Trail difficulty:	More difficult
Surface quality:	Single and double tracked
Food and facilities:	Rentals, lessons, retail shop, on-site restaurant Traditions (open Friday through Sunday and vacation weeks), snacks in the shop and at Rob's Hut on trail system (weekends and vacation weeks). Nearby is the Follansbee Inn on Kezar Lake in North Sutton (800–626–4221) for overnights.
Phone numbers:	The Norsk Cross-Country Ski Center at the Lake Sunapee Country Club can be reached at (800) 426-6775.

"Norsk" is Scandinavian for "from Norway." Though Norway is far from the Lake Sunapee area, the spirit is right there at Norsk. The touring center hasn't been around as long as the hearty Vikings, but for more than a quarter century skiers have been skiing the rolling trails of the Lake Sunapee Country Club golf course, abutting private lands and a nature preserve. All of these trails bask in the shadows of 2,937-foot-high Mount Kearsarge to the south.

The center opened in 1976 under the auspices of John and Nancy Schlosser. At that time, there were only seven trails along a 10-mile network. Since then it has grown to more than 32 miles of groomed lanes. After twenty-four years at the center, the Schlossers handed over the reigns to John and Maureen Chiarella, a couple immersed in the ski business as college racers, coaches, and ski area administrators.

Cascade Loop
Scale: 1:14,000 or 4.5" = 1 mile

Since its beginnings in 1976, a few things have changed. Some trails have been tweaked, snowshoes are allowed (on two trail areas: the Zinger Network and The Low Plain Natural Area, which includes several trails), and leashed dogs can follow along only on the North Flats Trail and the Zinger/Low Plains Areas. The uniqueness of Norsk is the large percentage of one-way trails that connect six hubs. At times going one way can be maddening (especially when there is a nice downhill to be had), but there is a flow to the trails. Ample signs make it easy for newcomers to Norsk to get around

The six hubs have different flavors. The North Woods section is both skate and classically groomed, with technically designed trails (lots of turns and transitions) for racing. The Sundown section is groomed for classic skiing, while Skater's Waltz has skate lanes. Zinger has a backcountry taste and Kearsarge is set for skaters and classic skiers.

Choices are many. Better skiers like to ride the aptly named Roller Coaster Trail to Rob's Hut on the Blackwater River, open on weekends, with its several bridge crossings and proximity to a frozen swamp. Large portions of the 3-mile-long Sundown trail bisect the Low Plain, Natural Area, a natural area with nesting boxes and habitat for moose, hare, and fox.

The Cascade Loop is a favorite among skiers for its winter views to Mount Kearsarge. The circuit itself is a rolling delight with a tad of uphill punishment and downhill reward. By taking the gentle South Trail, which skirts the edge of the golf course and glides through a stand of pines, skiers get the chance to warm up before heading into the woods along an easy section of the Sundown Trail. The Tango Trail means it is time to use those herringbone skills before linking up to Cascade, which has that backwoods feel to it. Cascade also passes by a choice home where no doubt every skier wants to live. Let those skis go on Otter Slide before heading to the flats of Pit Road and then the cover of the woods along the Spruce Trail, which will get skiers back to the golf course for the gentle return to the beginning.

Directions at a glance

0.0 Leave touring center on South Trail.

0.5 Turn left on Sundown.

1.3 Bear right on Tango Trail.

1.4 Bear right on Tango Trail.

2.0 Bear left on Cascade Loop.

2.2 Bear left on Cascade Loop.

2.4 Turn right on Cascade Loop.

4.2 Bear right on Cascade Loop.

4.3 Bear left on Cascade Loop.

4.4 Straight on Otter Slide.

4.8 Turn right on Pit Road.

4.9 Turn left on Sundown.

5.0 Turn right on Spruce Trail.

5.5 Right on Kearsarge.

5.7 Bear right on South Trail back to touring center.

How to get there

From I–89, exit 11, in New London, turn onto Country Club Lane from Route 11. The touring center is on Country Club Lane.

Holts Ledge
Lyme, New Hampshire

Type of trail:	
Also used by:	Hikers
Distance:	2.2 miles round-trip
Terrain:	Climb through forest to fenced-in ledge with mountain vistas
Trail difficulty:	Easy to moderate
Surface quality:	Unpacked
Food and facilities:	Before the trek, the Lyme Country Store on Route 10 in Lyme can supply snacks and sandwiches. With the trailhead's proximity to Hanover and Dartmouth College, there are a number of inns to select. About 4 miles from the Dartmouth Skiway on Route 10 in Lyme is the Loch Lyme Lodge (800–423–2141) while the 200-year-old Alden Country Inn (800–794–2296) is on the way to the trailhead along Dorchester Road in Lyme. The Dartmouth Skiway, with its ski-area food and prices, is the closest cup of hot chocolate for after the hike or head back to the pub at the Alden Country Inn for lunch. The Skiway doesn't have snowshoe rentals but does have water and rest rooms in the new base lodge.
Phone numbers:	The Hanover Area Chamber of Commerce, (603) 643–3115. The Dartmouth Outing Club, (603) 646–2428.

The ferns and wildflowers are long gone during a New Hampshire winter. Depending on the amount of snow, ancient stone walls peek out from winter's snowy blanket. Through the maple and birch forests the trail leads to a fenced-in ledge with the mountains of New Hampshire and Vermont beyond the drop-off.

Holts Ledge, across the road from the Dartmouth Skiway, is a year-round outdoor destination for all creatures. During the nonsnow months, peregrine falcons nest in the steep, rocky ledges. During the snow months, snowshoers emerge from the silence of the woods to gaze out from the ledge and hear the blasting snowguns on the nearby trails of the

Holts Ledge

Scale: 1:11,060 or 1" = 1 mile

BM 874

Grant

START/ FINISH

APPALACHIAN TRAIL

1200

1300

Trapper John Shelter

SKI LIFT

SKI LIFT

1600

Ledge

TRAIL

Holts

N

Skiway. Downhill skiers and snowboarders exit a lift not too far from the ledge. It's best not to snowshoe on the ski trails.

The ubiquitous Appalachian Trail (AT) is the way to the ledge. There is the familiar white blaze that hikers from Maine to Georgia know all too well. There is also the orange blaze of the Dartmouth Outing Club, which maintains some 70 miles of the AT, including the section to the ledge. The DOC is steeped in history since its 1909 inception. It was and is a pioneering force in New England outdoor recreation, from organizing skiing expeditions to Tuckerman Ravine to participating in the lavish Dartmouth Winter Carnival.

The Appalachian Trail is also a winter path to adventure.

The snowshoe trek to Holts Ledge is not exactly easy. But it is close to it. There are a couple of moderate pitches to remind you the hike isn't flat. Additionally, a few easy brook crossings remind snowshoers to pay attention to the trail.

The trail begins with a gradual climb up a hill through the woods, providing some respite from the wind should it be blowing. Nearly a half mile into the adventure, a side trail leads right to the Trapper John lean-to, a primitive structure. A stream crossing is next before you climb up a hill to the ledge. The AT turns to the right, but a side trail leads left to a more open area. Heed the fences. Venturing beyond them may appear to be a short way down, time wise, but because of the steep ledge, chances are it may be your last snowshoe trip too. The side trail also leads to the ski trails. From the Ledge, which is about 2,100 feet in elevation, there are vantage points to mountains like Smarts in the north, Kearsarge to the east, and Vermont's Ascutney to the south.

How to get there

From Route 10 in Lyme, turn onto Dorchester Road by the white Congregational church. Travel approximately 3.3 miles, first passing through the village of Lyme, to the trailhead on the right-hand side. Roadside parking is limited so it's best to travel about 100 yards and park by the Dartmouth Skiway.

Directions at a glance

0.0 From trailhead, follow Appalachian Trail south.

0.6 Continue on AT south as spur trail to shelter enters right.

1.1 Turn left for ledges.

Return via same route.

Battery Seaman Loop

Odiorne Point State Park, Rye, New Hampshire

Type of trail:	
Also used by:	Walkers
Distance:	Nearly 2.0 miles
Terrain:	Flat seaside stroll or ski
Trail difficulty:	Easiest
Surface quality:	Ungroomed, but skier tracked
Food and facilities:	Odiorne Point State Park and the Seacoast Science Center are adjacent to each other. Both charge small admission fees. No facilities are available in the park, but rest rooms and water are available at the center. There is a shopping center located at the junction of Routes 1 and 1A in Portsmouth for last minute lunch items. Yoken's Restaurant (603–436–8224) is a landmark seacoast restaurant and the light's always on at Portsmouth's Motel 6 (603–334–6606).
Phone numbers:	New Hampshire Division of Parks and Recreation, (603) 271–3556; Seacoast Science Center, (603) 436–8043.

The crashing of waves against the rocky shore and the invigorating smell of the sea are not elements usually associated with snowshoeing and cross-country skiing. On a trip to Odiorne Point State Park in Rye, visitors not only get a taste of the sea, but nature and history as well. The park and Seacoast Science Center sit side by side. If the chill of winter is too cold, head inside to the exhibits to learn about Odiorne's role in United States history, the placement of fortifications around the point in World War II, or the nature of tidepools. Perhaps your visit will coincide with a lecture, children's story hour, or scavenger hunt.

Be forewarned about snow conditions on the seacoast. A thaw can melt the snow quickly. It's not unusual for visitors to end up walking instead of heading out on skis.

Odiorne Point, on 300 acres of coastline, was made a state park in 1961. Here is where fishermen from Scotland landed in 1623 to establish one of the first European settlements in the country. When World War II began, Fort Dearborn was built at the point to protect Portsmouth Harbor from possible attack. The batteries remain where the military pointed their huge guns toward the sea.

The trail network in the park is not well signed. But there are plenty of landmarks and interpretive panels that make doing this loop an easy task.

The loop begins just around to the right by Battery 204, where massive shells are left out for display next to picnic tables. You'll see the battery when driving into the park. Park your car to the right. Then head over behind the tollbooth and follow the road with the sign that says BUS PARKING.

The trail begins to the left by a few large rocks and wooden trees. Head in through the thicket of trees. The trail takes a left. Look out on the waters where snow meets the sea. The trail hugs the shoreline and offers many views of the lighthouse in the distance. A couple of trails enter from the right. Ignore them. The trail swings to the left away from the shore. It's nice and wide.

At about 0.5 mile bear right through a grove of trees. There is a marsh through the trees on the right. Soon, you pass the Battery Seaman. Head in and explore. But it's just graffiti. The trail heads to the right as you pass a second part of the battery. At the far side of the battery, look out at the boats and docks. A trail to Frost Point enters right. Take it and loop around. At the point interpretive signs detail the history of and add a bit of insight into the life of a beach inhabitant—the sandworm. The sandworm, usually found along the coast in mud or sand, is generally used as fishing bait.

Complete the loop and continue straight ahead to the other side of the battery, built in 1942. Shoot straight down through the wide, flat trail. Pass the battery and then keep an eye out for a World War II structure on the left. (It is filled with graffiti and not worth stopping for).

The trail then intersects a bike path by a fence and gate. Turn left. The path parallels Route 1A. It will pass a fresh water pond on the left, where you'll find more interpretive signs. The straight shot continues to the park entrance. Here a left takes you back to the first battery and the parking lot.

Directions at a glance

0.0 Leave the parking area through the posts and rocks.

0.5 Bear right by the fresh water marsh and soon see the Battery Seaman.

0.8 Bear right to Frost Point and follow the loop.

0.9 Continue straight and go past the other side of the Battery Seaman.

1.2 Turn left onto bike path by fence and gate.

1.7 Turn left by park entrance.

1.8 Turn right, back to parking lot.

How to get there

From the Portsmouth Traffic Circle, exit via Route 1 Bypass south to Route 1. Turn left at the lights with Elwyn Road (sign points to Route 1A). At Foyes Corner go straight through at the stop sign to Route 1A. Follow Route 1A to Odiorne State Park Fort Dearborn site and turn left.

Heald Pond Trail

Wilton, New Hampshire

Type of trail:	
Also used by:	Hikers
Distance:	2.0 miles
Terrain:	Flat loop around a pond with numbered stations for facts about nature
Trail difficulty:	Easiest
Surface quality:	Ungroomed, skier tracked
Food and facilities:	No facilities here, so bring all you need to eat and drink. After the jaunt try the Peterborough Diner (603–924–6202) on Depot Street. The Greater Peterborough Chamber of Commerce (603–924–7234) can help with lodging, while Eastern Mountain Sports (603–924–7231) has rentals.
Phone numbers:	Society for the Protection of New Hampshire Forests, (603) 224–9945; for emergencies, 911.

Heald Pond is a delight to explore in winter. It is an easy snowshoe or ski through red maple, white pine, and hemlock. The pond itself offers fine views of Fisk Hill. Its twenty-five numbered identification stations along the way make the 2-mile trek go faster. The Pond Loop is very well marked with yellow blazes. The trail goes near the pond's edge, an apple orchard, beaver lodge, and stone wall.

The sixty-nine-acre pond is part of the Heald Tract, a preserve of the Society for the Protection of New Hampshire Forests. The land was donated in 1986 and has grown to encompass 500 acres with about 6 miles of walking and hiking paths. The property straddles Wilton and Temple and is such an excellent spot for introducing children to the natural world that the fourth graders of Wilton Elementary School in 1987–88 wrote a small guide to go along with the numbered stations (offered by the Society for the Protection of New Hampshire Forests). The trek is not diminished without the guide. But here we'll try and give some information that the children have shared.

The Pond Loop is directly across the parking area and is marked with a yellow blaze. The trail continues to the pond and bears right over a drainage into the woods. Here you'll see the first of the markers. Journey along the stations on the flat trail. The first ten identify red maple, white pine, mountain laurel, partridge berry, hemlock, elm, witch hazel, red oak, a den tree, and the decay of a log.

Pass the stone wall built from rocks left from glaciers and bear left into an open field that then reenters the woods. Just after station 14,

A horse takes hay from a snowshoer.

Directions at a glance

0.0 Follow the Pond Trail.

0.6 The Ledge Trail enters from the right, but continue straight on the Pond Trail.

0.7 The Look-See Trail enters left. Turn right and continue on the Pond Trail.

1.0 The Ledge, Spring, and Fisk Hill Trails enter. Turn right on the Pond Trail.

1.2 Turn right on the Ledge Cut-off Trail.

1.5 Turn left on the Pond Trail.

1.9 Cross the road back to the parking area.

which details fungus on a birch tree, travel over a narrow footbridge and enjoy the walk along the shore. There is a beaver lodge to see. Continue along the pond's edge and look for the orchards and an abandoned farm. Head back into the woods and cross another narrow footbridge. The Look-See Trail soon enters from the left. It's a short walk to the shores of the pond for a look and see. Continue left on the Pond Trail. Soon you'll have a stone wall to follow and stepping stones to help you through a wet area.

The blue-blazed Fisk Hill Trail enters after station 25.

Stay on the Pond Trail. The path widens and climbs for just a short spell. It is very quiet here. The Pond Trail gives way to the right. Choose the Ledge Cut-off. The climb continues a bit more but then descends and winds past huge, flat rock ledges.

The trail comes out at a junction with the Pond Trail. Turn left on the Pond Trail. If those snowshoe imprints or ski tracks look familiar, they could be yours. You have been here before.

Retrace your steps along the Pond Trail and enjoy the solitude.

How to get there

From Peterborough or points west, take Route 101 east to Route 31 south in Wilton and turn right. From the Nashua area take Route 101 west to Route 31 south in Wilton and turn left. Travel 2.5 miles and turn right on King Brook Road. At 0.9 mile turn left on Kimball Hill Road. It's a short 0.1 mile to a right on Heald Road. Follow the road 0.3 mile and park at the second plowed area after the HEALD TRACT SOCIETY FOR THE PROTECTION OF NEW HAMPSHIRE FORESTS sign on the right. The Pond Trail leaves from the parking area across the road. Parking is limited to a couple of vehicles.

Bear Brook State Park Loop

Allenstown, New Hampshire

Type of trail:	
Also used by:	Hikers, portions by snowmobilers, dogsledders
Distance:	5.0 miles
Terrain:	Rolling ski or snowshoe outside the state capital
Trail difficulty:	Easiest
Surface quality:	Ungroomed, single tracked, double tracked
Food and facilities:	Primitive toilets are located at the trailhead parking area and at a few places along the loop. There is a shelter just off the loop that makes a fine stop for lunch overlooking Smith Pond. No camping is allowed. No water is available during the loop. As for food the best bet is at the junction of Routes 3 and 28 in Allenstown. There is a grocery store and a restaurant, Chantilly's. Rentals are at Eastern Mountain Sports (603–224–8781) in Concord. The Concord Chamber of Commerce (603–224–2508) can suggest lodging.
Phone numbers:	For an emergency, 911; for information on Bear Brook State Park, call the New Hampshire Division of Parks and Recreation, Trails Bureau, (603) 271–3254.

The beauty of Bear Brook State Park is that there is something for everyone. With nearly 10,000 acres of forest, there is room for the snowshoer, cross-country skier, snowmobiler, and even the dogsledder. At times they may cross each other's path, but for the most part the networks are separate.

The loop through Bear Brook utilizes several different trails—Little Bear, Bobcat, Broken Boulder, and Pitch Pine. Tie them all together and you have quite an enjoyable bundle. Birch, pine, red oak, and hemlock trees make up much of the forest you'll be passing through. There are also a few clearings, areas of downed trees off the trails, and "snags," dead standing trees left for wildlife to use. For example, woodpeckers eat the insects found in these trees. Commercial timber sales have taken place in the park, and signs up near the beginning of the loop explain what has taken place in the area. You'll spot (deer scat) and hear (fluttering of a game bird taking off) evidence of wildlife. Trail conditions can vary tremendously with the amount of snowfall and season.

A rustic shelter that overlooks the marshy Smith Pond is a good place to rest and have a bite to eat. It's not too many trails that cross through an archery range, and this loop does, skirting Archery Pond and the targets used by archers in the nonsnow months.

Circular blue signs bearing the letters *XC* mark the trails and blue arrows point the way. Every once in a while you'll pass a number that is just an indicator of where you are according to the state maps available at the trailhead.

Leave the parking lot on the Little Bear Trail, zip down, and turn left at the sign for the Little Bear Trail. The trail is wide and rises gently. New growth pine, tree stumps, and snags are evidence of a December 1996 logging operation. Posted signs explain what happened.

Directions at a glance

0.0 From parking area leave via the Little Bear Trail.

0.1 Turn left on Little Bear Trail. The Bear Brook Trail goes straight.

0.4 Bear left on the Little Bear Trail.

1.5 Stay straight on the Bobcat Trail by the XC 9 sign.

2.0 Stay straight on the Bobcat Trail at XC 14.

3.0 Turn left on the Broken Boulder Trail at XC 7.

3.5 Bear left on Broken Boulder at XC 6.

4.2 Turn right by the archery range at XC 3 on Pitch Pine Trail. Follow it 0.8 mile to the parking area.

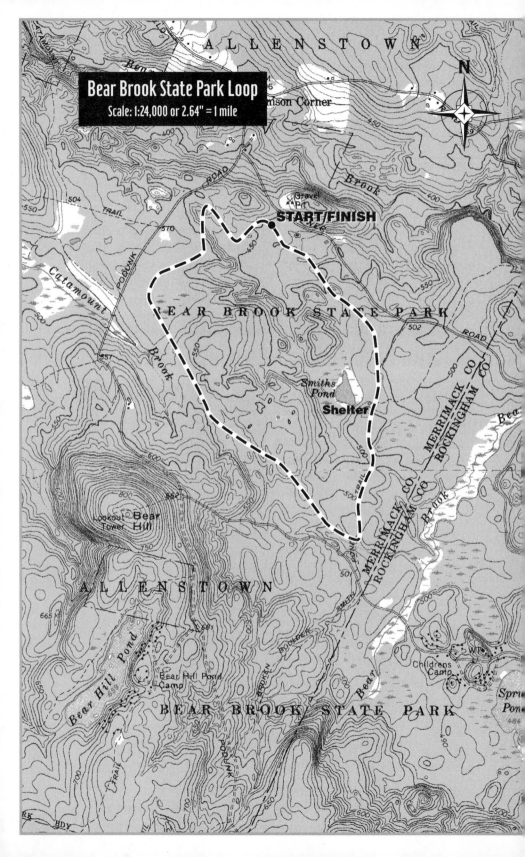

Bear Brook State Park Loop
Scale: 1:24,000 or 2.64" = 1 mile

START/FINISH

Shelter

Little Bear Trail bears to the left and starts climbing along a hill. The trail narrows and winds upward. There is a bit of relief with a few rolling sections. Snake around a big sand pit and enjoy the ride before coming to a green gate where the trail crosses a snowmobile path (Hayes Farm Trail). Little Bear continues straight and gently slopes downward. Pass some toilets and come out at a summer parking area. Stay to the left and look for the blue XC signs. Turn left by the sign that says XC 9 and points to the Chipmunk and Bobcat Trails. The path is the Bobcat Trail. Skirt the marsh. Tall evergreens appear to stand guard to welcome your arrival. The Bobcat is an easy grade. There will be several trail junctions that are easy to follow for the rest of the loop. Bobcat is a straight shot and wide for some time. Flat rocks line the road at times. Take notice of the leaves that have turned brown but have not yet fallen. Bobcat bears hard to the left before a long, rollicking downhill. Turn left on the wide Broken Boulder Trail at the junction (XC 7). Soon the path to the Smith Pond Shelter leaves left. It's a good rest spot.

Stay on Broken Boulder as it winds down. Broken Boulder bears left at the junction with the Pitch Pine Trail and goes around the pond.

Cross over Podunk Road and stay straight on Broken Boulder. Continue the decent, cross a snowmobile trail, and enjoy the winding descent. You'll soon cross the only bridge.

A tunnel of small evergreens leads to signs of the archery range. At the clearing turn right and head down through the range on the edge of Archery Pond, by the targets, toilets, and picnic tables.

The trail undergoes a personality change after this—it becomes schizophrenic. It's a winding roller coaster and crosses various snowmobile paths and a gravel pit in an area of a November 1996 timber cut. But this lasts only a short while because the end of the loop is in sight. Broken Boulder now becomes the Pitch Pine Trail. Stay with it until the end. There are a couple of buildings up ahead. Near them, head back down to the parking area where the loop began.

How to get there

Take I–93 to exit 13. Travel on Route 3 south to Route 28 north in Allenstown. Turn left and travel about 3.0 miles to a sign at the entrance to Bear Brook State Park. This is the Allenstown-Deerfield Road. Turn right at the sign and travel 3.2 miles to Podunk Road. Turn right on Podunk Road and travel 0.3 mile to skier parking area on right.

Mount Monadnock Loop

Monadnock State Park, Jaffrey, New Hampshire

Type of trail:	⬭, portions for ▬▬▶
Also used by:	Hikers
Distance:	4.6 miles
Terrain:	Flat to steep with Monadnock views for experienced snowshoers
Trail difficulty:	Most difficult, easiest portion for CC
Surface quality:	Ungroomed
Food and facilities:	Monadnock State Park is open year-round but is staffed only on weekends and holidays during winter. Winter camping and pit toilets are available. Bring your own water midweek. On weekends and holidays a ranger staffs the park store from 8:30 A.M. to 4:30 P.M. There visitors can get the latest snow conditions and trail information and stock up on last-minute food items. As of 1998 rangers collected a day-use service charge of $2.50 per adult. During the week there was no ranger collecting. Pets are prohibited year-round. For those visiting during the week, maps are available at the toll booth. For a late lunch try the Rusty Bucket Cafe (603–532–4101) on Main Street in Jaffrey. Rentals are at Summer's Backcountry Sports (603–357–5107) in Keene.
Phone numbers:	Monadnock State Park manager, (603) 532–8862; New Hampshire State Police, (800) 525–5555; for medical emergencies, 911.

Mount Monadnock is the crown jewel in southwestern New Hampshire's treasure—Monadnock State Park. At 3,165 feet Monadnock's rocky summit is arguably the most climbed mountain in the world. More than 40 miles of hiking trails surround it, and in winter some 14 miles of ungroomed cross-country skiing is available. Keep in mind that snowshoes do not belong on the treeless summit with inadequate snow cover.

The snowshoe loop suggested here is not up the mountain but on its southern flank, on trails once walked by Emerson and Thoreau. This loop is only for the most experienced snowshoers. Crampons are a must. Wooden snowshoes without crampons will not suffice.

The terrain moves quickly from flat to steep with the narrow Cliff Walk trail aptly named. From its heights the views extend south to Gap Mountain and southeast to Wachusett in Massachusetts, east to the Wapacks, and southwest to Mount Greylock. But in winter, portions of

Cliff Walk can become icy and in a couple of spots glissading would be helpful to navigate the rocky outcrops. Those unfamiliar with the mountain should wait a few days after a snowfall so that footprints in the snow can show the way to the upper reaches, especially between the Point Surprise and Hello Rock section of Cliff Walk. The elevation rises from about 1,300 feet to 2,300 feet.

As for the ski trails at the base of the mountain, they are primarily old logging roads, bridle paths, and summer hiking trails—all ungroomed. Six to ten inches of snow are needed for adequate skiing.

The Parker Trail, on which the snowshoe loop begins, is a beginner ski trail. It can be snowshoed, too. Put skis on after crossing the footbridge and ascend the forested trail by the reservoir fence. Note the frozen drips of ice and the waterfall. The ski or snowshoe is 1.5 miles out to the Old Toll Road. Take it back for a 3.0-mile excursion. The trail is blazed in yellow. It is lined in part by portions of an old stone wall that once was part of a road to Keene. There are a few wet drainage areas to negotiate. At 0.6 mile the Lost Farm Trail enters from the right. Huge boulders soon come into view. The boulders were plucked from the south side of the mountain when a glacier moved through. The Cliff Walk Trail enters from the right 0.5 mile later. It's another 0.4 mile to the Old Toll Road (a plowed road), which once led to a hotel that stood from 1860 to 1954. Return the same way, enjoying the descent.

> ## Directions at a glance
>
> 0.0 From the trailhead to the Parker Trail, head over the footbridge and along the trail.
>
> 0.6 Turn right on the Lost Farm Trail.
>
> 1.8 Head straight when you reach Cliff Walk.
>
> 2.1 Point Surprise Trail enters from the right. Stay left.
>
> 2.3 Turn right on Hello Rock Trail.
>
> 2.5 Turn left on Old Toll Road.
>
> 3.1 Turn left on Parker Trail and follow it 1.5 miles to the park headquarters.

The snowshoe loop begins at the Parker Trail trailhead, too. Follow it and link up to the Lost Farm Trail by turning right at 0.6 mile. The Lost Farm Trail ascends, sometimes steeply, near huge fallen boulders. The trail is blazed in white, while the stone wall follows a blue blaze. The forest changes to evergreens. Look out at the views of neighboring Massachusetts.

As the trail nears Cliff Walk, rocks and ice unite. Caution: Watch for icy stretches now. Follow the Cliff Walk to the left for awe-inspiring beauty. The edge of the trail plunges dramatically. Look for a sign out by the rocks that says AINSWORTH SEAT, named after Rev. Laban Ainsworth, the first settled minister of Jaffrey, who purchased 200 acres south of the summit in 1784.

After the Ainsworth Seat the trail enters the trees again and drops quickly through a pair of rocks, where glissading might be a good idea, to a junction with the Point Surprise Trail. There is a sign. Stay left on Cliff Walk for another shot at the ledges. The trail descends steeply again to a junction with the Hello Rock Trail. Two huge, beefy boulders mark the crossing. Turn right on the Hello Rock Trail and return to the trees. Soon a tunnel of pines provides a thoroughfare to a clearing.

The Cliff Walk Trail descends steeply to the left. It is not recommended as a snowshoe trail to those unfamiliar with the area.

Soon you'll spot a couple of buildings through the trees. This is by the Halfway House Site, where a hotel once stood. Now it is a private residence. Hello Rock is a pleasant jaunt downward. A clearing provides a bit of relief. The Hello Rock Trail continues to the left as the Thoreau and Point Surprise Trails enter from the right. Shortly enter the Halfway House Site clearing. Here one sign points to the White Arrow Trail, another to Hedgehog, Noble, Do Drop, and Side Foot Trails. Interestingly enough turn left on the obvious Old Toll Road, which is not signed initially. Head down a few yards and pass a sign that points to the Old Halfway House Trail.

Respect the sign that says PRIVATE and continue down the plowed road for about 0.6 mile and then turn left on the yellow-blazed Parker Trail. The trail descends for most of its way back to the parking lot at the park headquarters.

How to get there

From Jaffrey travel on Route 124 west, through Jaffrey Center. Turn right on Dublin Road at 2.3 miles where a sign points to Monadnock State Park. Follow Dublin Road 1.4 miles to Poole Road, where you'll see another sign for Monadnock. Turn left. You reach a plowed parking area by making a left after the tollbooth. This is parking lot number one. At the far end of the parking area is a plowed road that goes to a second parking area. Here parking is limited. The trailhead is reached by making a left at the fence surrounding Poole Reservoir. A sign marks the beginning of the trail.

Kilburn Loop
Pisgah State Park, Hinsdale, New Hampshire

Type of trail:	▬▬▬ ⬭⬭⬭
Also used by:	Hikers
Distance:	6.4 miles
Terrain:	Flat to rolling excursion in the shelter of a wooded park
Trail difficulty:	Easiest to more difficult
Surface quality:	Ungroomed
Food and facilities:	There are no facilities on this excursion. Stock up on food in Hinsdale and Chesterfield, on opposite ends of Route 63. It is very important to bring plenty of food and fluids if you are planning to do the entire loop. Nearby Keene has rentals (Summer's Backcountry Sports, 603–357–5107) and lodging (Chamber of Commerce is 603–352–1303).
Phone numbers:	Pisgah State Park, (603) 239–8153; New Hampshire State Police, (800) 525–5555.

With more than 13,500 acres of forest, the twenty-one square miles of Pisgah State Park make it the largest property in the New Hampshire State Park system. The park is located in the southwestern corner of the state, not far from Brattleboro, Vermont, or the Massachusetts border. Seven ponds, four highland ridges, and several wetlands are all protected by the park, located between the small towns of Chesterfield and Hinsdale.

Miles of trails meander through the park. Some are part of the state's snowmobile corridor system, while others are open to multiple use, including the snowmobile. The six trailheads that lead into the park offer many options, but the Kilburn Loop is for human-powered vehicles only.

The Kilburn Loop itself is a 5.0-mile-long loop through evergreens, beech, hemlock, and occasional maple. You'll spot a trio of beaver ponds through the woods, and part of the trip skirts the western shores of the quiet Kilburn Pond. You can travel on it in either direction, but we prefer to save the level grades along the pond's shores for the end of the tour, instead

> ### Directions at a glance
> 0.0 From the trailhead take Kilburn Road 0.7 mile.
> 0.7 Bear slightly left on Kilburn Loop.
> 0.8 Turn right and cross bridge.
> 1.4 Bear right as Pisgah Mountain Trail enters from the left.
> 5.7 Bear left back on Kilburn Road to trailhead.

of the beginning. For those skiers and snowshoers looking for a shorter outing, this too can be had. Instead of taking the loop clockwise, as suggested here, take it just a mile or so counterclockwise, find a secluded spot along the rolling bank, have a bite, and head back.

Begin by leaving the well-marked trailhead. The trail, called Kilburn Road, is wide at this point and will soon dip down to the pond. Look for the work of the pileated woodpecker among the trees. It's not that hard to find.

The road heads down to a junction. Those just seeking a pondside picnic can head right and scoot back after dessert. The rest of us, turn left at the sign that reads KILBURN LOOP, and we will save views of the pond for later in the day.

This sheltered romp through the forest is blazed with blue diamonds. At about 0.1 mile from the junction, the trail turns to the right over a bridge with handrails. Notice the darkness once through the evergreens. Though winter, it's warm and cozy in here. The trail begins to ascend. Take a look around and notice the patterns of nature in the snow. Pine cones, pine needles, and other markers left by Mother Nature make the trail a gallery of natural spin art.

The trail rolls up and down, sometimes steeply. Up on the right, it climbs to a ridge from the forest floor. The Pisgah Mountain Trail enters from the left, but bear right and see the sign that says PISGAH LOOP 4.3. There are flat and narrow sections here, too. A yellow caution sign is your signal for a nice winding downhill.

The trail snakes to the left and heads through a bit of a boulder field, covered in snow, trees and their roots wrapped around the rocks. Head down and peer through the trees on the left to see a beaver pond. The trail heads up to the right again, sometimes steeply. Listen closely for the music of winter's songbirds.

Darkness gives way to light as the beech and hemlock hold court. The noon sun leads the way. Head down a gentle grade and snake around a ledge. Corn snow tops the crust as the sun beats down. The corn is a harbinger of playful months to come.

Up and down you go. When you come to a footbridge, the trail turns to the right. At the left is a beaver pond. The trail widens and heads up. Then down it goes again, a long, pleasant downhill. It then bears to the right. You cross a bridge and another long ascent begins. Cross one more bridge (look for the old bridge to the left) and continue on up.

You'll hear the rushing waters of Kilburn Brook. Slide down and come to a fourth bridge, a narrow span by yet a third beaver pond.

The roller coaster continues. High up on a ridge, then come down to gaze on the shore of Kilburn Pond. Follow its shores along the water's

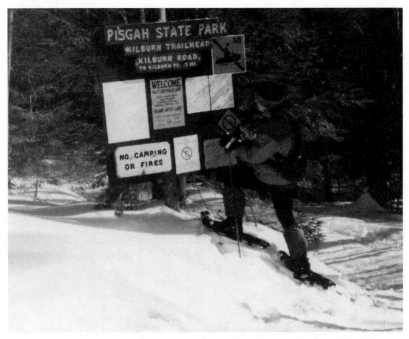

A snowshoer reads the signs at the entrance to Pisgah State Park and the start of the Kilburn Pond Loop.

edge. Sometimes it can be marshy there. If you want, find your own way to the ice.

Stay with the trail and come to the sign that says KILBURN LOOP again. Bear left and climb for the last time. See the trailhead.

Rejoice!

How to get there

From I–91 in Vermont take exit 3 to New Hampshire Route 9. Travel 6.0 miles. Make a right on Route 63 and travel about 4.5 miles south, through the village of Chesterfield. The Kilburn Road trailhead to Pisgah State Park is on the left. From Hinsdale take 63 north about 4.0 miles. The trailhead is on the right.

Appendix

VERMONT SKI CENTERS

The following are cross-country skiing areas in Vermont:

Blueberry Hill
Goshen, VT 05733
Phone: 802–247–6735
E-mail: info@blueberryhillinn.com
Web: www.blueberryhillinn.com

Blueberry Lake Cross Country
Warren, VT 05674
Phone: 802–496–6687

Bolton Valley Touring Center
Bolton, VT 05477
Phone: 802–434–3444
Web: www.boltonvalleyvt.com

Burke Mountain Cross Country
753 Pinkham Road
East Burke, VT 05832
Phone: 802–626–8338
E-mail: bam@together.net
Web: www.burkemtn.com

Catamount Family Center
592 Gov. Chittenden Road
Williston, VT 05495
Phone: 802–879–6001
E-mail: abbie@catamountoutdoor.
    com
Web: catamountoutdoor.com

Churchill House Inn
Brandon, VT 05733
Phone: 802–247–3078
Web: www.churchillhouseinn.com

Craftsbury Outdoor Center
Craftsbury Common, VT 05827
Phone: 800–729–7751
Web: www.craftsbury.com

Edson Hill Manor
1500 Edson Hill Road
Stowe, VT 05672
Phone: 802–253–8954
Web: www.stowevt.com

Equinox
Union Street
Manchester Village, VT 05254
Phone: 802–362–4700
Web: www.equinoxresort.com

Grafton Ponds
Townshend Road
Grafton, VT 05416
Phone: 802–843–2400
Web: www.old-tavern.com/
    recreation

Green Trails Inn and Cross Country
    Center
Brookfield, VT 05036
Phone: 802–276–3412
Web: www.greentrailsinn.com

Hazen's Notch Association
Montgomery Center, VT 05471
Phone: 802–326–4799
Web: www.pbpub.com

Hermitage Cross Country Touring
    Center
Coldbrook Road
Wilmington, VT 05363
Phone: 802–464–3511
Web: www.hermitageinn.com

Highland Lodge
Caspian Lake Road
Greensboro, VT 05841
Phone: 802–533–2647
E-mail: hlodge@connriver.net
Web: www.highlandlodge.com

Jay Peak Ski Touring Center
Jay, VT 05859
Phone: 802–988–2611
Web: www.jaypeakresort.com

The Landgrove Inn
Landrove, VT 05148
Phone: 802–824–6673
Web: www.landgroveinn.com

Meadow Brook Inn
Route 11
Landgrove, VT 05148
Phone: 802–824–6444
Web: www.meadowbinn.com

Merck Forest and Farmland Center
Rupert Mountain Road
Rupert, VT 05768
Phone: 802–394–7836
E-mail: merck@vermontel.com
Web: www.merckforest.com

Mountain Meadows Cross Country
Killington, VT 05751
Phone: 800–221–0598
E-mail: mtmxc@sover.net
Web: www.xcskiing.net/

Mountain Top Cross Country Ski
    Resort
Mountain Top Road
Chittenden, VT 05737
Phone: 802–483–6089
Web: www.mountaintopinn.com

Okemo Valley Nordic Center
77 Okemo Ridge Road
Ludlow, VT 05149
Phone: 802–228–1396
Web: www.okemo.com

Ole's Cross Country Center
Airport Road
Warren, VT 05673
Phone: 802–496–3430
E-mail: jthvt@madriver.com

Prospect Mountain Cross Country
    Ski Center
Route 9
Woodford, VT 05201
Phone: 802–442–2575
Web: www.prospectmountain.com

Rikert's Ski Touring Center at
    Middlebury College
Ripton, VT 05766
Phone: 802–388–2759
Web: www.middlebury.edu

Round Barn Farm
1661 East Warren Road
Waitsfield, VT 05673
Phone: 802–496–2276
E-mail: info@innatroundbarn.com
Web: www.innatroundbarn.com

Sleepy Hollow Inn Ski and Bike
   Center
1805 Sherman Hollow Road
Huntington, VT 05462
Phone: 802–434–2283
E-mail: info@skisleepyhollow.com
Web: www.skisleepyhollow.com

Stratton Mountain Cross Country
Stratton, VT
Phone: 802–297–4114
Web: www.stratton.com

Smugglers' Notch Resort
Smugglers' Notch, VT 05464
Phone: 802–644–8851
E-mail: smuggs@smuggs.com
Web: www.smuggs.com

Sterling Ridge Cross-Country Center
Jeffersonville, VT 05464
Phone: 802–644–8265
E-mail: vtcabins@sover.net
Web: www.virtualvermont.com/
   sterlingridge/

Stowe Mountain Resort
5781 Mountain Road
Stowe, VT 05672
Phone: 802–253–3688
Web: www.stowe.com

Sugarbush Resort
Warren, VT 05674
Phone: 802–583–2605
Web: www.sugarbush.com

Three Stallion Inn
Lower Stock Farm Road
Randolph, VT 05060
Phone: 800–424–5575
Web: www.3stallioninn.com

Timber Creek
Wilmington, VT 05363
Phone: 802–464–0999
Web: www.sover.net/~vtcxcl

Topnotch Touring Center
4000 Mountain Road
Stowe, VT 05672
Phone: 802–253–8585
E-mail: info@topnotch-resort.com
Web: www.topnotch-resort.com

Trapp Family Lodge
700 Trapp Hill Road
Stowe, VT 05672
Phone: 802–253–5719
Web: www.trappfamily.com

The Viking Nordic Center
Londonderry, VT 05148
Phone: 802–824–3933
Web: www.vikingnordic.com

Wilderness Trails
Clubhouse Road
Quechee, VT 05059
Phone: 802–295–7620
E-mail: wildernesstrails@aol.com
Web: www.scenesofvermont.com/
   wildernesstrails

Woodstock Ski Touring Center
Woodstock, VT 05091
Phone: 800–448–7900
E-mail: email@woodstockinn.com
Web: www.woodstockinn.com

White House
Route 9 East
Wilmington, VT 05363
Phone: 800–541–2135
Web: www.whitehouseinn.com

Wild Wings Ski Touring Center
Peru, VT 05152
Phone: 802–824–6793
Web: www.linkvermont.com

NEW HAMPSHIRE SKI CENTERS

The following are cross-country skiing areas in New Hampshire:

The Balsams
Route 26
Dixville Notch, NH 03576
Phone: 800–255–0600
E-mail: thebalsams@aol.com
Web: www.thebalsams.com

Bear Notch Ski Touring Center
Route 302
Bartlett, NH 03812
Phone: 603–374–2277
Web: www.bearnotchski.com

Bretton Woods
Route 302
Bretton Woods, NH 03575
Phone: 603–278–3322
E-mail: info@brettonwoods.com
Web: www.brettonwoods.com

Eastman Cross Country Center
Exit 13 off I–89
Grantham, NH 03753
Phone: 603–863–4500
E-mail: eastmanrec@srnet.com
Web: www.eastman-lake.com/
    winter.html

Franconia Village Cross Country
Route 116
Franconia, NH 03580
Phone: 800–473–5299
E-mail: info@franconiainn.com
Web: www.franconiainn.com

Great Glen Trails Outdoor Center
Route 16
Pinkham Notch, NH 03581
Phone: 603–466–2333
E-mail: greatgln@mt-washington.
    com
Web: www.mt-washington.com

Gunstock Cross-Country and
    Snowshoe Center
Route 11A
Gilford, NH 03246
Phone: 800–GUNSTOCK
E-mail: gunstock@gunstock.com
Web: www.gunstock.com

Jackson Ski Touring Foundation
Main Street
Jackson, NH 03846
Phone: 800–XC–SNOWS
E-mail: info@jacksonxc.org
Web: www.jacksonxc.org

King Pine Cross-Country
Route 153
East Madison, NH 03849
Phone: 800–373–3754
E-mail: info@purityspring.com
Web: www.purityspring.com

Loon Mountain Cross-Country
Route 112
Lincoln, NH 03251
Phone: 603–745–8111
E-mail: info@loonmtn.com
Web: www.loonmtn.com

Mount Washington Valley Ski
    Touring and Snowshoe Center
Route 16
Intervale, NH 03845
Phone: 603–356–9920
E-mail: info@crosscountryskinh.com
Web: www.crosscountryskinh.com

Nordic Center at Waterville Valley
Town Square
Waterville Valley, NH 03215
Phone: 603–236–4666
E-mail: info@waterville.com
Web: www.waterville.com

Nordic Skier
Routes 28/109
Wolfeboro, NH 03894
Phone: 603–569–3151
E-mail: info@nordicskiersports.com
Web: www.wolfeboroxc.org

Norsk Cross-Country
Route 11
New London, NH 03257
Phone: 800–426–6775
E-mail: info@skinorsk.com
Web: www.skinorsk.com

Phillips Brook Backcountry
    Recreation Area
Paris Road
Stark, NH 03582
Phone: 800–TRAILS8
Web: www.phillipsbrook.org

Windblown Cross-Country
Routes 124/123
New Ipswich, NH 03071
Phone: 603–878–2869
Web: www.skinh.com/windblown

Woodbound Inn
62 Woodbound Road
Rindge, NH 03461
Phone: 800–688–7770
E-mail: woodbound@aol.com
Web: www.nhweb.com/wood-
    bound/index.html

RESOURCES

The following are resource organizations for snowshoeing
and cross-country skiing in Vermont and New Hampshire:

American Hiking Society
P.O. Box 20160
Washington, DC 20041-2160
Phone: 301–565–6704
Web: www.americanhiking.org

Appalachian Mountain Club
5 Joy Street
Boston, MA 02108
Phone: 617–523–0636
Web: www.outdoors.org

Catamount Trail Association
1 Main Street, Suite 308A
Burlington, VT 05401
Phone: 802–864–5794
E-mail: ctamail@aol.com
Web: www.catamounttrail.
    together.com

Cross Country Ski Areas Association
259 Bolton Road
Winchester, NH 03470
Phone: 603–239–4341
Web: www.xcski.org

Dartmouth Outing Club
Dartmouth College
Hanover, NH 03755
Phone: 603–646–2428
Web: www.dartmouth.edu/
    student/doc/

Green Mountain Club
4711 Waterbury-Stowe Road
Waterbury Center, VT 05677
Phone: 802–244–7037
E-mail: gmc@greenmountainclub.org
Web: www.greenmountainclub.org

Green Mountain National Forest
Forest Supervisor's Office
231 North Main Street
Rutland, VT 05701
Phone: 802–747–6700
Web: www.fs.fed.us/r9/gmfl

New Hamphire Department of
    Travel and Tourism Development
P.O. Box 1856
Concord, NH 03302
Phone: 603–271–2343
Web: www.visitnh.gov

New Hampshire Division of Parks
    and Recreation
P.O. Box 1856
Concord, NH 03302
Phone: 603–271–3556
Web: www.nhparks.state.nh.us

Ski New Hampshire
P.O. Box 10
North Woodstock, NH 03262
Phone: 800–887–5464
E-mail: info@skinh.com
Web: www.skinh.com

Ski Vermont
P.O. Box 368
Montpelier, VT 05601
Phone: 802–223–2439
Web: www.skivermont.com

Squam Lakes Association
P.O. Box 204
Holderness, NH 03245
Phone: 603–968–7336
Web: www.squamlakes.org

Vermont Department of Forests,
Parks and Recreation
103 South Main Street
Waterbury, VT 05676
Phone: 802–244–8711
Web: www.state.vt.us/anr/fpr/
index.htm

Vermont Association of Snow
Travelers
41 Granger Road
Barre, VT 05641
Phone: 802–229–0005
Web: www.vtvast.org

Vermont Department of Tourism
and Marketing
134 State Street
Montpelier, VT 05602
Phone: 802–828–3237
Web: www.travel-vermont.com

White Mountain National Forest
Supervisor's Office
719 North Main Street
Laconia, NH 03246
Phone: 603–528–8721
Web: www.fs.fed.us/r9/white/

Bibliography

The following books are valuable resources:

Appalachian Mountain Club. *AMC White Mountain Guide* (26th ed.). Boston, 1999.

Gange, Jared. *Hiker's Guide to the Mountains of New Hampshire.* Huntington, Vermont: Huntington Graphics, 1997.

Gange, Jared. *Hiker's Guide to the Mountains of Vermont.* Huntington, Vermont: Huntington Graphics, 1997.

Goodman, David. *Backcountry Skiing and Snowboarding Adventures: Classic Backcountry Tours in Maine & New Hampshire.* Boston: Appalachian Mountain Club, 1999.

Green Mountain Club. *Day Hiker's Guide to Vermont* (3rd ed.). Waterbury Center, Vermont, 1987.

Green Mountain Club. *Long Trail Guide* (24th ed.). Waterbury Center, Vermont, 1996.

Mudge, John. *The White Mountains: Names, Places and Legends.* Etna, New Hampshire: The Durand Press, 1992.

Preston, Philip. *The Squam Trail Guide.* Holderness, New Hampshire: Squam Lake Association, 1991.

Smith, Steve D. *Ponds and Lakes in the White Mountains.* Woodstock, Vermont: Backcountry, 1990.

Tilton, Buck, and Hubbell, Frank. *Medicine for the Backcountry.* (3rd ed.) Guilford, Connecticut: The Globe Pequot Press, 1999.

About the Author

Marty Basch is a writer, lecturer, and adventurer who has written widely on outdoor recreational themes. He has written five books, including *Winter Trails Vermont and New Hampshire,* which won an Honorable Mention at the 1999 National Outdoor Book Awards. His articles have appeared in publications such as *The Boston Globe* and *Ski,* and his syndicated outdoor adventure column can be found in several New England newspapers. He has won awards from the Associated Press for his radio reporting and the Harold Hirsch Award from the North American Snowsports Journalists Association for his ski writing.

An avid long-distance bicyclist, Basch has gone on several radical rides, including a 5,198-mile solo journey in 1994 from Maine to Alaska, chronicled in his first book, *Against the Wind.* A 3,000-mile solo cycling trip near and above the Arctic Circle in 1996 was chronicled in *Above the Circle.* He has also written *The White Mountain Ride Guide* and *Winter Trails Maine.*

Marty Basch lives in New Hampshire's White Mountains.